COOKING WITH CRIMESPREE

COOKING WITH CRIMESPREE

EDITED BY
JON & RUTH JORDAN

Compilation Copyright 2014 by Jon & Ruth Jordan
First Edition: October 2014

All rights reserved. No part of the book may be reproduced in any form or by any electronic or mechanical means, including information storage and retrieval systems, without permission in writing from the publisher, except by a reviewer who may quote brief passages in a review.

Down & Out Books
3959 Van Dyke Rd, Ste. 265
Lutz, FL 33558
www.DownAndOutBooks.com

Cover design by JT Lindroos
Photos by Erica Ruth Neubauer

ISBN: 1937-4958-2-5

ISBN-13: 978-1-937495-82-4

We'd like to dedicate this to everyone who has ever fed us or eaten with us.
—Jon & Ruth

Foreword

We met at a mystery convention. Surprise, a large part of our life now is in some way related to our love of mystery and crime fiction. A lot of our friends today share our passion for everything criminal. More friendships have developed because of Crimespree. There's another commonality in most of our friendships.

FOOD! When we started dating we discovered that we both really enjoy cooking. It's a natural that we started cooking for friends. We started dining with friends. We sent out care packages of coffee, cookies, chocolate and received oodles in return. Whether the annual Murder and Mayhem dinner or inviting an author touring on the road for a home cooked meal and a glass of wine, Castle Crimespree has seen its share of dinner parties over the years. Just as delightful are the meals we've had out with our fellow mystery lovers both in Milwaukee and throughout the states. There's nothing quite like taking the time for a good meal and great conversation.

We would never have met if not for Ian Rankin inviting us both for a drink. Laura Lippman might not be such a good friend if it weren't for the Calzones at Louisa's. Dan and Kate Malmon might have been mostly alright with meeting us in person for the first time in a restaurant but I doubt they would have come to our house—Dan is cautious but he loves hugs. Nothing says love quite like Sharon Lynch's Chicago Mix Popcorn. Reed Farrel Coleman making Guacamole in our kitchen? Robert Crais did our dishes. The meals over the years have been amazing. We smile at the thought of how many have been shared with Judy Bobalik, Dave Bieman and Richard Katz.

It was a natural evolution to include a recipe on the last page of Crimespree. A wink and a nod to a demographic of mystery readers and writers we dearly love. Because we all read and sometimes make the recipes at the back of the books, right?

COOKING WITH CRIMESPREE

We've been running recipes in the magazine for a while and it seemed like a good idea to take this to the next step. We hope you enjoy these recipes and the company you are with when you eat and drink. Salute!

Salute!
—Jon & Ruth

"This is my advice to people: Learn how to cook, try new recipes, learn from your mistakes, be fearless, and above all have fun"
—Julia Child

"If more of us valued food and cheer and song above hoarded gold, it would be a merrier world."
—J.R.R. Tolkien, author of the Lord of the Rings trilogy

BREAKFAST

"I went to a restaurant that serves 'breakfast at any time' so I ordered French toast during the Renaissance."
—Steven Wright

Joe Pickett's Mad Scramble Breakfast
CJ Box

This recipe is an experiment of my own that started one way but has resolved into something else. The nice thing about the "Mad Scramble" is that it is good either at home or over a campfire in the Wind River Mountains or elsewhere. I've cooked it for fellow author/fishermen and have been rewarded by hearty grunts from people like Jeff Parker and Brian Wiprud. Another nice thing about it is that it takes a while to cook, so by the time it's ready everyone is starved and thinks it's better than it actually is. I also like it because it contains one of the most sadly neglected of the essential food groups—Tater Tots. Next to chicken thighs, Tater Tots don't get their proper due. I've tried real baked potatoes, boiled potatoes, packaged hash browns—and none of them taste as good as Tater Tots. I'm still pissed with Ore-Ida for no longer making Tater Tots with Onion, but that's another story.

Ingredients:
1 bag frozen Ore-Ida Tater Tots with Onion
1/8 cup olive oil
4 tablespoons minced garlic
1/2 diced green pepper
1/4 pound minced ham or Canadian bacon.
Or sausage. Or pastrami. Or all of them.
6 to 8 eggs
Seasoned salt
Pepper

Preparation:
Pour the thawed Tater Tots into a large skillet with at least half of the olive oil already beginning to smoke at medium-high. As the potatoes cook, break them up into the consistency of oat

meal and turn them often, always adding a little more oil. It should take twenty to thirty minutes for the potatoes to become crisp. Season with seasoned salt and pepper. Don't be shy.

While the potatoes cook, break 6 eggs into a bowl and scramble. Add in the minced garlic, green pepper, and ham or bacon.

When the potatoes are golden brown, pour the egg mixture in. Whip the egg mixture to mix thoroughly with the potatoes, constantly turning and chopping with a spatula until the eggs are completely cooked. The green peppers should just be softening.

Pour the whole scramble into a serving bowl and serve with tick buttered toast, Jalapeno sauce and ketchup.

VARIATION: Sometimes, rather than scrambling in the eggs I add all of the ingredients to the potatoes except the eggs, which I fry or poach on the side. I cover the plate with the potatoes and serve the eggs on top.

ANOTHER VARIATION: Drizzle homemade Hollandaise sauce (3 egg yolks, 2 tablespoons lemon juice and water, 1/2 stick melted butter, blended with dashes of salt and pepper) over the scramble and serve. This variation is especially healthy and good for the heart and arteries.

Ellie Hatcher's Lazy Nutella Breakfast
Alafair Burke

Readers of the Ellie Hatcher novels may have noticed that the NYPD Detective doesn't cook. She eats, but she doesn't cook. The closest she comes to cooking is ordering takeout or dipping her spoon in an ever-handy jar of Nutella. But even Ellie can handle a breakfast that requires nothing but three ingredients, a knife and, if you're feeling fancy, a toaster.

Serves one, because that's how Ellie Hatcher rolls. And if you have to ask for help figuring out how to double, triple, or quadruple this recipe, Ellie would say there is no hope for you.

Ingredients:
  1 English muffin
  Nutella
  Half a banana—sliced

Preparation:
Split the English muffin in half. Toast it to your liking if you're feeling motivated to cook.
   Slather each half liberally with Nutella. Top with banana slices. Serve open-faced. Lick fingers when finished.

Sausage Gravy and Eggs
Jon Jordan

This is a recipe I played around with and managed to end up making just the way I liked it. I cooked for a Mother's Day one year for both my parents and my in-laws. We didn't eat again until the next day. I can't bake so I either use Bisquick for the biscuits or more often I substitute toast.

Ingredients:
- A package of link sausage (about ten)
- A package of patties (about 8)
- A tube of breakfast sausage (I like Jimmy Dean's Sage flavored)
- Milk
- Flour
- Eggs
- Sourdough bread

Preparation:
Cook the link and patty sausages together, cook the tube sausage in a second pan. When patties and links are almost done drop heat way down and drain into second pan with tube sausage. When tube sausage is done, break it up into small pieces and slowly add a bit of flour and milk until your gravy starts to form. Sprinkle a little paprika in and a bit of pepper.

Cook eggs the way you like, I prefer over easy. Make a few pieces of sourdough toast, pour gravy over toast. Set eggs on gravy, sausages on the side and eat!

The World's Greatest Waffle
Barry Lancet

Those who know I wrote *Japantown* and *Tokyo Kill* may be surprised to see a non-Japanese recipe here, but I couldn't pass up the opportunity to share what I consider a tremendous dish. Which happens to be Belgian, I believe.

My fallback was fugu, the highly poisonous blowfish to which diners in Japan succumb to from time to time. I did contemplate sharing instructions for preparing the fish, but as the method is far from foolproof for the untrained, and as Crimespree's intention is to increase readership rather than decimate it, I decided to forgo fugu for now. Maybe next time.

This waffle is brilliant. It is lightness itself, with a slight tanginess. So give it a shot. I am not sure where the recipe originated, but it has appeared in a booklet that comes with some Waring waffle irons. I suspect the true origin lies somewhere in a Belgian kitchen.

This version has the added advantage of having been tested and refined numerous times by my brother Marc, who is quite handy in the kitchen when he is not teaching art, throwing pots, or building sculpture. My contribution is also extensive: I tasted every version of the waffle he offered up at the breakfast table.

Most of the mixing for these waffles is done the night before. In the morning, just add in the eggs, vanilla, and baking soda while the waffle maker is heating. These waffles can also be made the morning of, as brother Marc has proven. If you have leftover batter, it may be covered and kept in the refrigerator for up to 3 days, or cook up the rest of the batter, freeze the extra waffles, and retrieve them for a quick gourmet breakfast. Frozen is not nearly as good as fresh, but it is light years beyond the store-bought variety.

COOKING WITH CRIMESPREE

Ingredients:
- 1/2 cup warm (105 degrees to 110 degrees) water
- 1 tablespoon sugar
- 2 1/4 teaspoons active dry yeast (1 packet)
- 2 cups whole milk, warm (about 105 degrees)
- 1/2 cup unsalted butter, melted and cooled
- 1 teaspoon salt
- 2 cups unbleached, all-purpose flour
- 2 large eggs, lightly beaten
- 2 teaspoons vanilla extract
- 1/4 teaspoon baking soda

Preparation:

The previous evening, or at least eight hours before you plan to make waffles, mix together the warm water, sugar, and yeast. Put aside the mixture for ten minutes, until it becomes foamy. Note: Use a thermometer, as temperature is critical to growing yeast. Lower than 105 degrees and the yeast will grow slowly. Higher than 110 degrees and you will kill the yeast.

Melt the butter in the milk as you heat it and then let rest until 110 degrees. Add the salt. If you keep a candy or meat thermometer close by, or whatever type you have at hand, monitoring the temperature is but a moment's work. Stir the warm milk, melted butter, and salt into the yeast mixture. Beat in the flour until the mixture is smooth. If you use a hand-mixer for this step, set it on low.

Cover the bowl tightly with plastic wrap and leave it overnight, or for at least eight hours. Do not refrigerate. Be sure to use a large bowl where the mixture fills no more than one-third of the bowl to avoid spillage when the yeast causes the batter to expand.

When you are ready to cook, preheat your waffle iron to a medium-high or preferred setting. (For exacting foodies, a less-detailed version of this recipe came with the Waring Pro Belgian Waffle Maker; setting #4 is preferred).

Leave the waffle iron to heat. To the batter, add the remaining three ingredients: the eggs, vanilla, and baking soda. When the iron is ready, pour in batter. Consider using a measuring cup to control the portion of batter introduced in the center of the waffle iron. Close cover and cook. For waffle irons with a pivoting mechanism, rotate 180 degrees, bake in the hot waffle maker until beeper sounds.

Repeat to make as many waffles as needed. They are best when served immediately, but can also be kept warm in an oven preheated to 200 degrees. Arrange waffles on a large tray or cookie sheet.

Set out toppings of your choice, including sliced fresh fruit in season, powdered sugar, a warmed maple or fruit syrup, jam, and whipped cream.

Barry Lancet's first thriller in the Jim Brodie series, Japantown, *was selected as a Best Debut of Year by Suspense Magazine and by renowned mystery critic Oline H. Cogdill in her annual roundup. It has also been shortlisted for a Barry Award and optioned by J. J. Abrams' Bad Robot Productions, in association with Warner Bros. The book was the result of more than two decades of living in Japan as an expat American. His work in Tokyo gave him inside access to many traditional and business circles most outsiders and Japanese are never granted.* Tokyo Kill *is the second offering in the Jim Brodie series. The third is on the way. Lancet is based in Japan, but visits the U.S. frequently. For more information, please go to http://barrylancet.com/ or look for Barry on Facebook and Twitter*

Quick Apple Pancake (Microwave)
Christine Matthews' easy bake kitchen

Ingredients:
- 1/4 cup butter or margarine
- 1 1/2 cups thinly sliced apples
- 1/2 cup sugar
- 1/2 teaspoon cinnamon
- 1/4 teaspoon nutmeg
- 1 teaspoon vanilla
- 1 cup Hungry Jack Complete or Buttermilk Complete Pancake Mix

Preparation:
Microwave butter in nine inch pie plate until melted. Stir in apples, sugar, cinnamon and nutmeg. Cover and microwave on high three to four minutes, until apples are tender.

In a medium bowl mix pancake mix, 1/2 teaspoon cinnamon, 1/4 teaspoon nutmeg, 3/4 cup water and 1 teaspoon vanilla. Pour over apples and top with 1 tablespoon sugar and 1/4 teaspoon cinnamon.

Microwave three to five minutes, until pancake is done. Let it set five minutes and serve inverted with topping of your choice.

APPETIZERS

"Appetizers, be they simple or complicated must deliver for they preview the meal."
—Anonymous

Caro's Good Dog Treats—One for your pet!
Sparkle Abbey

Recipe from the Pampered Pets mystery series by Sparkle Abbey.

Carolina Lamont, animal lover and former Texas beauty queen, moved to California after a very nasty and public divorce. With eleven thousand dogs—more dogs than kids—Laguna Beach seemed like the perfect spot to open a pet therapy business. And it had been, up until she had to catch a killer by the tail. Whether dealing with misbehaving canines or murder suspects, Caro always keeps a few of her homemade dog treats on hand.

Here's Caro's recipe:

First, preheat your oven to 350 degrees.

In a big bowl, combine all the ingredients with just enough water to make it the consistency of cookie dough.

You'll need:
- 1/2 cup of creamy unsalted peanut butter
- 1 cup oat flour
- 1 cup brown rice flour (Caro uses organic)
- 1 egg
- 1 tablespoon of honey
- 1/2 cup finely grated carrot (Dogbert , Caro's dog, loves carrots)

Optional: You can also add cooked bacon, a bit of grated cheese, or other ingredients for flavor, but don't add too much or it will mess with the consistency of the dough, and cause your treats to fall apart.

Once you've got your treat dough all stirred up, put it between pieces of parchment paper and roll it out to about 1/4-inch thickness. Then cut the dough with a cookie cutter. You can use whatever shape strikes your fancy. Caro often uses dog bone shapes of different sizes. Next, put them on a regular cookie sheet and bake them between fifteen and twenty minutes or until they're golden retriever brown.

Let them cool and then put them in an airtight container. You can store your Caro's Good Dog treats for about a week (or you can freeze them for later use) but keep an eye on them. There are no preservatives, so watch out for spoilage.

This makes a couple of dozen treats so there's plenty to go around. Please share them with your dog.

Sparkle Abbey is the pseudonym of mystery authors Mary Lee Woods and Anita Carter. They write the national bestselling pet mystery series which features two feuding cousins who solve whodunits set in the wacky world of pampered pets, precious pedigrees, and secrets. The two authors chose to use Sparkle Abbey as their pen name because it combines the names of their two rescue pets, Sparkle (Mary Lee's cat) and Abbey (Anita's dog).

Spinach Balls
CJ Carpenter

Ingredients:
    2 boxes of chopped drained spinach
    2 cups of bread crumbs
    1 cup parmesan cheese
    6 eggs beaten
    12 tablespoon softened butter
    Dash of salt and pepper and nutmeg

Preparation:
Roll into small balls.
Ten minutes in the oven at 350 degrees.
Serve with choice of mustard.

Big Bang Guacamole
Catherine Coulter

Prepare to become the expert in the most outstanding guacamole in the known Universe. Indeed, this recipe is even footnoted *In A Hitchhiker's Guide to the Galaxy* (well, it should have been). In my FBI series, Special Agents crowd into the Savich and Sherlock living room on football Sundays to chow down S&S's superb guacamole. (I start salivating when writing these scenes.) I personally can't pass an entire four quarters of football without stuffing my face. So follow my easy perfect instructions and make your reputation. Don't forget, avocados are one of the top fifteen perfect foods so this wonderful green creation is blessed by nutritionists everywhere.

What you need:
  2-3 very ripe avocados
  Lemon Juice
  2 Roma tomatoes
  Lots of scallions (or purple onion if you prefer)
  1 tablespoon non-fat sour cream
  Salt/pepper/garlic salt to taste
  3 drops of Tabasco sauce
  Dollop of Miracle Whip Lite
  Primavera Tortilla Chips

Putting the BB ingredients together:
Mash avocados, immediately add lots of lemon juice.
Cut up tomatoes and wring out all juice, add to mashed avocado.
Cut up onions small, add to mashed avocado.
Add salt, pepper, garlic salt, sour cream, Tabasco sauce, TASTE, and add whatever if you deem necessary.

Always have both a man and a woman taste—and then you decide.

Add a dollop of Miracle Whip Lite, not too much, just enough to makes mixture smooth, lighten the color a bit.

Heat Primavera tortilla chips in hot oven, 400 degrees, maybe up to five minutes but watch carefully, add salt.

Turn on NFL Football and SERVE.

WALLOW IN BLISS.

P.S. Eating guacamole and chips while reading one of my books could be even better.

Sharon's Salsa
Sharon Lynch

Ingredients:
    1 15-ounce can black beans, drained
    1 1/2 cup frozen corn
    1 chopped red pepper
    2 chopped medium tomatoes
    1/2 cup chopped red onion
    1/2 cup chopped fresh cilantro
    2 thinly sliced jalapeno peppers
    1/3 cup olive oil
    1/3 cup lime juice
    1 teaspoon salt
    1/2 teaspoon cumin

Mix and serve with tortilla chips.

Crack Pretzels
Erica Ruth Neubauer

Ingredients:
1 regular size bag of pretzel sticks (or mini pretzels)
1 teaspoons cayenne pepper
1 teaspoons lemon pepper
1 1/2 teaspoons garlic powder
1 package hidden valley ranch dry mix
3/4 cup canola oil
1 gallon zip lock baggie

Directions:
Put pretzels in a gallon zip lock bag. Mix cayenne pepper, lemon pepper, garlic powder, ranch seasoning and canola oil together. Pour mixture over pretzels in zip lock baggie. Let mixture and pretzels sit for several hours, or overnight if possible. Spread out on large baking sheet. Bake at 200 for forty minutes.

I always bag them the night before, let them soak overnight and cook them the next morning.

La Ristra Guacamole
Twist Phelan

Ingredients:
- 1 large avocado, pitted, peeled, and diced
- 1-2 tablespoons diced Roma tomato
- 1 tablespoon diced red onion
- 1 tablespoon seeded and diced jalapeno pepper
- 1 tablespoon freshly chopped cilantro
- Juice from half of a lime
- Sea salt and fresh-cracked pepper to taste
- 1 tablespoon pomegranate arils (seeds)

Directions:
Mix avocado, tomato, onion, jalapeno, and cilantro.
Squeeze lime juice over the mixture.
Sprinkle with salt and pepper to taste; mix gently.
Add pomegranate arils; fold together gently. Mixture will be chunky.
Transfer to a dip bowl and serve immediately with tortilla chips (preferably homemade)
Makes four servings.

Homemade tortilla chips

Ingredients:
- Tortillas
- Vegetable oil

Directions:
Cut several tortillas into four pieces each.
Heat a little vegetable oil in a fry pan.
Place tortilla pieces in the pan and cook until crisp.
Drain on a paper towel.

La Ristra is a Pinnacle Peak tradition. Known for its modern Southwestern cuisine, the restaurant's signature dishes include the house guacamole, made special by the addition of tart/sweet pomegranate seeds. My character Hannah Dain always orders the chunky delight when at La Ristra with her on-again/off-again boyfriend, Cooper Smith. And she isn't embarrassed to beat him to the last scrape of the bowl!

Buffalo Tofu Wings!
Tom Schreck

I'm a half ass vegetarian who longs for good bar food. The condition: the bar food can't be made out of a mammal. My invention—Buffalo Tofu Wings!

Here's what you need:
  12 ounces of extra firm Tofu, drained and pressed
  Frank's Red Hot sauce
  2 tablespoons of margarine
  KC Masterpiece Original BBQ sauce
  2 Basset Hounds
  1 Bloodhound
  3 overweight cats
  Crumbly Bleu Cheese
  Wishbone Bleu Cheese dressing
  Garlic
  Pepper
  1 wife
  Carrots and celery
  12-pack of Schlitz

Directions:
Turn on the Fry Daddy home Fry-o-later. Open a Schlitz. Mix one cup of Frank's Red Hot, the margarine, the BBQ sauce and a splash of Schlitz in a large mixing bowl. Immediately drink the remainder of the Schlitz can. Go into the living room and see why the bassets are barking out the window and to remove the loafer from the bloodhound's mouth. Yell loudly. Disregard the hounds' ambivalence.

Throw empty Schlitz away and open a fresh one. Mix the bleu cheese dressing with bleu cheese crumbles, pepper and garlic. Listen to the wife's day while the two bassets bark and the bloodhound bays. Curse at cat for scratching sofa. Finish beer and open new one.

Cut tofu into chicken wing size strips. Pull basset hound heads out of carrot and celery serving dish and yell, "Fuck!" Apologize to wife. Discard beer.

Open Fry Daddy cover and wipe scalding splattering grease from face. Sip from fresh beer. Dump Tofu chunks into greasy mixture and close cover. Sprint to rescue cat attacked by three hounds. Yell, "Fuck!" as shin is cracked on coffee table. Apologize to wife. Finish beer.

Remove tofu from fry-o-later when they are the consistency of Styrofoam packing chips, mix in hot sauce preparation and dip in bleu cheese. Hold aloft from snapping scent hounds and enjoy

Best served with a cold Schlitz. Or two.

Tom Schreck is the author of IMBA Best Seller On the Ropes, *IMBA Killer Selection* TKO *and the forthcoming* Out Cold.

Three-Layer Fiesta Dip
L.J. Sellers

Party food needs to be visually appealing and look like you put a lot of work into it. Much like the cover of a book! This dip does all that, but only takes a few minutes and one bowl that you rinse out between layers. The best food dishes also have multiple flavors that you taste distinctively and simultaneously, and this dip does that too—much like my complex plots. A great crowd pleaser for your book club.

The only mystery in this recipe is how a party dip this delicious and attractive can be so easy to make.

Bottom layer:
Large can of refried beans, small can of diced green chilies, salt to taste
Blend the ingredients together in a bowl, then spread with a spatula on a party platter. (Rinse the bowl with hot water and reuse for next layer.)

Middle layer:
Pint of low-fat sour cream and half a package of taco seasoning
Whip the two ingredients together in a bowl. Drop spoonfuls of the seasoned sour cream all over the bean layer, then gently spread it, leaving an edge of the bean layer showing. (Rinse the bowl with hot water to reuse for next layer.)

Top layer:
Guacamole.
You can use store bought guacamole, your own recipe, or make an easy version by blending two avocados with three tablespoons of your favorite salsa.

Drop the guacamole by spoonfuls, then gently spread it, leaving an edge of the sour cream layer showing.

Garnish the top with colorful additions. My favorite combination is finely diced black olives, finely diced red onion, and grated sharp cheddar cheese. The only hard part is keeping people out of the dip until guests arrive.

L.J. Sellers writes the bestselling Detective Jackson mystery series—a two-time Readers Favorite Award winner—as well as provocative standalone thrillers. Her novels have been highly praised by reviewers, and her Jackson books are the highest-rated crime fiction on Amazon. L.J. resides in Eugene, Oregon where her novels are set and is an award-winning journalist who earned the Grand Neal. When not plotting murders, she enjoys standup comedy, cycling, social networking, and attending mystery conferences. She's also been known to jump out of airplanes.

A Taste of Alan Furst's Central Europe
Erin Ferretti Slattery

One of the reasons I love reading Alan Furst's historical espionage series is that it takes me back to familiar sights, sounds, and flavors I enjoyed when living and working in Europe (not as a spy, I should note). Furst's landscapes and characters are drawn with economy—one or two details, sounds, or typical local traits stand in for the larger whole, and *Kingdom of Shadows* (Random House, 2000) offers some of the best examples of Furst's style. In this novel, the hero, Nicholas Morath, is pressed into service by his uncle, Count Polanyi, a Hungarian diplomat, to help with international resistance to Hitler's advances across Europe. As the novel opens in Paris, 1938, Morath leaves behind his day job, advertising; his Argentinean lover, Cara; and his regular enjoyment of French cuisine and wine. Yet even as the novel changes one country for another as the plot accelerates, food remains a subtle but notable presence, often functioning as more than mere scene decoration.

The fictional Brasserie Heiniger in Paris makes an appearance, as it does in each of these novels, and Cara plans a lavish picnic from Fauchon, but when Morath is working, there's rarely the clink of wine glasses and fine china. Food in *Kingdom of Shadows* usually appears at the periphery, but the culinary details add touches of color, light, normalcy, tradition, and a sense of stability in the ever-shifting war-time Europe of the novel. Furst often references a local dish to drop readers fully and simply into a new setting, as he does early in the novel, when Morath travels to Uzhorod (in modern-day western Ukraine) to meet a contact. In Morath's eyes, Uzhorod is another place growing dog-eared at the edges after passing through centuries of territorial squabbles. As he defines it: "Ruthenia. Or, affectionately, Little Russia. Or, technically,

Sub-Carpathian Ukraine. A Slavic nibble taken by the medieval kings of Hungary, and ever since a lost land in the northeast corner of the nation. Then, after the world war, on a rare day when American idealism went hand in hand with French diplomacy [...] they stuck it onto Slovakia and handed it to the Czechs." (42)

The owner of the small hotel where Morath is staying in Uzhorod serves him a meal that, like Furst's description, echoes the cultural blurring and layering that's occurred in the region, over time: "jellied calf's foot, buckwheat groats with mushrooms, white cheese with scallions, and thin pancakes with red-current [sic] jam." (43) It's not fancy, but it suits the setting, and Morath compliments the innkeeper on the meal.

Both the simple meal above and one that appears later, a luxurious classic Czech dinner of roast goose, red cabbage, and dumplings served in Morath's honor at a Czech officers' mess, are foods that appear at kitchen tables and on restaurant menus across the region today. In the spirit of celebrating Furst's attention to food and culture, here's an easy but unique Czech recipe that works well as a weekend snack with rustic wheat bread and Pilsner (or dark beer, or your favorite beer).

Nakládaný hermelín (Marinated Cheese)
Serves 4-6 as an appetizer

Ingredients:
2 rounds of Camembert
Sliced garlic (2-3 cloves per Camembert round)
Rosemary
Thyme
Allspice
Juniper berries (15 per Camembert round)
Equal parts pepper and sweet paprika
1 large yellow onion, thinly sliced
1 red onion, thinly sliced
1 red bell pepper, thinly sliced
1 green bell pepper, thinly sliced
A small handful of bay leaves
Vegetable oil (preferably sunflower oil)

Preparation:
This recipe requires advance preparation, preferably of at least two days. You'll also need a clean half-liter jar with a clamp (or airtight) lid. (A washed and dried pickle jar works well in a pinch.)

Using a sharp knife, slice each round of cheese in half horizontally and scatter the garlic over each half.

Next, sprinkle each half with the rosemary, thyme, allspice, juniper, pepper, and sweet paprika. Replace the top half of each cheese round and gently press the top half onto the bottom half to secure them together.

In the bottom of the jar, scatter a thin layer of onion, bell peppers, and bay leaves. Unless you're using a very wide-mouthed jar, you'll probably have to slice the cheese—still sealed together—into quarters or wedges. Add one layer at a time. (In the Czech Republic, you'll often see enormous jars of these sitting on the end of a bar, with five or six Camembert rounds in each layer.)

Continue layering Camembert wedges and vegetable slices, packing the contents in but without squashing them completely. Add the vegetable oil until the contents of the jar are submerged. Seal and refrigerate for at least forty-eight hours before serving with beer and bread.

(Food-safety note: Foods containing refrigerated garlic in oil should be consumed or disposed of within a week.)

Erin Ferretti Slattery lives and writes in New York. She is a member of MWA and Sisters in Crime. When she lived in Prague from 2006-2008, she worked for Rebo Publishers and taught at Charles University.

SOUPS

"I live on good soup, not on fine words."
—Moliere

Shrimp Brie Soup
Avery Aames

Inspired by Chef Purdhomme

How many of you have visited New Orleans? It's such a treat. Yes, the city is still suffering from the effects of Hurricane Katrina, but the spirit of the city and its people are strong, and the food and atmosphere incomparable.

When I visited, I was lucky enough to attend a luncheon at Chez Paul (Paul Prudhomme's restaurant in the French Quarter.) Highlights of the day included not only good music and good conversation but the artwork on the walls. Beside my table was whimsical artwork that included a recipe scrawled across it for Oyster Brie Champagne Soup. I jotted it down. When I returned home, I realized the recipe was intended for an entire restaurant. I've tweaked recipes before, but this was a challenge. May I share with you what turned out to be a fabulous soup: Shrimp Brie soup. Ah, to brie or not to brie?

Ingredients:
(serves 6-8)
- 1/2 cup unsalted butter
- 1/2 cup potato starch (potato flour)
- 4 cups vegetable stock
- 2 1/2 cups whipping cream
- 1 teaspoon white pepper
- 2 teaspoons salt
- 1/2 cup green onions (green tails only, about 1 bunch), diced
- 1 cup dry champagne
- 1 pound bay shrimp
- 4 ounces Brie, room temperature, rind removed

COOKING WITH CRIMESPREE

Directions:
In a 3-quart saucepan, over medium heat, melt butter.
Add potato starch and stir. Heat three minutes.
Add vegetable stock and stir. Heat three minutes.
Add whipping cream and pepper and salt and stir. Heat five minutes. (Stir occasionally to prevent cream from boiling).
Remove from heat.
Add champagne (will bubble), shrimp, and diced green onion tips.
Let stand ten minutes and pour into 6 to 8 bowls.
Adorn with slivers of Brie. Enjoy!

Cincinnati Chili
Laura Benedict

Measure into Stock Pot:
- 1 15ounce can Tomato Sauce
- 4 15 ounce cans Dark Red Kidney Beans
- 4 quarts water
- 5 tablespoons chili powder
- 1 teaspoon garlic powder
- 1 teaspoon dried oregano
- 1/4 teaspoon cloves
- 1/4 teaspoon cinnamon
- 1/4 teaspoon cumin
- 1/4 teaspoon allspice
- Dash of cayenne pepper
- 1/2 pound ground beef, browned and drained. (Can substitute ground turkey, but, really, it's not the same. If you do, add more cayenne pepper.)

Bring to a boil. Lower heat and simmer about 1 1/2 hours to desired thickness, stirring frequently. Local chili parlors serve it very thin, but it sticks to the noodles better if it's thicker.

Prepare:
1 package spaghetti according to package directions.
Serve topped with shredded Colby or Cheddar cheese and chopped onion.
Serves 6-8

Brooklyn Black Bean Soup
Reed Farrel Coleman

Ingredients:
  2 quarts chicken stock or water
  1 28 ounce can of black beans
  1 15 ounce can of black beans
  1 14.5 ounce can stewed tomatoes or peeled tomatoes
  1 half pound chorizo or kielbasa
  1 large yellow onion
  1 carrot
  2 celery spears
  6 cloves of fresh garlic
  1 dried chipotle chile
  1/4 teaspoon Anch chile powder
  1/2 teaspoon sea salt
  1/2 teaspoon fresh cracked pepper
  1/2 teaspoon dried oregano
  2 tablespoons olive oil

Preparation:
Place dried chipotle in a sauce pan with two cups of boiling water for ten minutes. Remove chipotle from water. Reserve water. Remove seeds and stem from pepper, taking care to keep your finger away from your eyes and other sensitive parts of your body. Slice chipotle. Slice chorizo into cubes. Remove beans from cans, place in a colander, and rinse. Brown in oil in a stock pot on high heat. Remove the sausage and add diced onion, carrot, celery, and garlic. Sauté veggies until slightly brown. Add back browned chorizo. Add sliced chipotle. Add half of the water reserved from cooking chipotle. Reduce by half. Add half of chicken stock and remainder of chipotle water. Reduce by one quarter. Add remainder of chicken stock, tomatoes, and beans. Add seasonings. Bring to a boil, cover,

and reduce to a simmer for thirty minutes. Skim for fat, taste for seasoning. Depending upon preference, you can serve as is or, as I prefer, hand-blended to a thick consistency, with many of the ingredients still discernable.

To serve:
Ladle soup into bowls about three quarters to the top. Add chopped cilantro for garnish. For a more formal presentation you can offer your guests several garnishes like chopped red onion, real bacon bits, sour cream, white rice.

Panicked Writer on Deadline Taco Soup
JT Ellison

On deadline? Pulling your hair out? Wishing someone else could stop and make dinner? Here's the perfect solution, a quick, healthy thirty minute meal that even the most stressed writer can throw together:

Ingredients:
- 2 pounds ground beef
- 1 1.25 ounce package taco seasoning mix
- 1 1/2 cups water
- 1 15 ounce can mild chili beans
- 1 15.25 ounce can whole kernel corn, drained
- 1 15 ounce can pinto beans, rinsed and drained
- 1 14.5 ounce can diced tomatoes
- 1 10 ounce can diced tomatoes with green chile peppers
- 1 4 ounce can chopped green chilies
- 1 1 ounce package ranch salad dressing mix
- Corn chips and sour cream for garnish (optional)

Directions:
In a Dutch oven or large kettle, cook beef over medium heat until no longer pink; drain.
Add taco seasoning and mix well. Stir in remaining ingredients.
Simmer, uncovered, for fifteen minutes or until heated through, stirring occasionally.
Serve with chips or add a dollop of sour cream.

I'm not a big fan of beans, so when I first had this at my book club, I only tried it out of politeness. But it's wonderful—filling and warm and spicy. And so quick! It's a go to meal when I've been writing all day and forget to make dinner. And yes, that happens a lot.

The Very Best Chicken Noodle Soup
JT Ellison

When it's cold season at the Ellisons, this delicious, hearty chicken noodle soup is just the ticket. I laugh every time I make it—I used to be so afraid of soups, and they're the easiest thing on the planet. This is my favorite: it's hearty, salty—good for sore throats—and filling. And you can easily double the recipe to serve a big family.

Ingredients:
- 3 large chicken breasts, cut into 2 to 3-inch pieces, seasoned generously with salt and pepper
- 2 tablespoons EVOO
- Standard Mire Poix—chop 1/2 half medium onion, 2 stalks of celery, and 2 large carrots
- 1 large clove garlic, minced
- 1 teaspoon dried thyme
- 2 bay leaves
- 1 package organic chicken stock
- 1 chicken bouillon cube (in 1 cup water)
- 1 1/4 cups of thin egg noodles
- 1 cup frozen sweet peas
- 2 teaspoons salt
- 2 teaspoons black pepper

Directions:

Cut chicken breasts into large pieces (2 to 3-inch pieces, about same thickness) and season generously with salt and pepper. Braise in olive oil until cooked through. Set aside.

In a large pot, heat olive oil on medium heat. Add the diced onion, celery and carrots. Sauté for about two minutes. Add in the garlic, thyme and bay leaves, cook until onions are translucent.

Return chicken to the pot. Stir so all the flavors mingle, add salt and pepper.

Add chicken stock, bouillon cube and water. Bring to a slow boil, then reduce heat to low. Simmer for thirty minutes.

Add peas and noodles, cook for ten minutes.

Serve with crusty French bread.

Red Hot Pepper Soup Cure (*)
Jamie Freveletti

So here's a great recipe for a soup that contains quite a few herbs with medicinal properties and which will come in handy during flu season. It's a delicious soup (but very, very spicy).

Ingredients:
- 1 head garlic
- 2 tablespoons olive oil
- 1 onion, chopped
- 4 bell peppers, any colors you like (I use red yellow and green to add color) seeded and chopped
- 2 jalapeno peppers seeded and chopped
- 3 tablespoons grated gingerroot
- 8 cups chicken broth
- 2 cups cooked shredded chicken (optional)
- 1 bunch cilantro, chopped
- Salt and Pepper
- Juice of 1 lemon

Preparation:
Instructions: Separate cloves of unpeeled garlic onto a baking sheet and bake at 350 degrees until soft, about fifteen minutes.

Cool, squeeze cloves out of their peels into a small bowl and mash with a spoon.

Heat the oil in a large soup pot. Add the onion and cook over low heat until tender, about ten minutes. Add the peppers, garlic and ginger and cook 1 minute. Add broth.

Add chicken if using salt pepper and lemon and simmer for about ten to twenty minutes.

(*) With thanks to the Chicago Tribune Magazine.

Murder and Mayhem Chili
Jon Jordan

Ingredients:
2 pounds pork—1/2-inch chunks
1 pound sausage—Italian or brats
3 pounds beef—1/2-inch chunks
1 pound bacon—pieces
1 tube chorizo
3 pounds hamburger
1 carrot
1 stalk celery
4 green pepper
6 onions
6-7 fresh tomatoes
3 cans chopped tomatoes
2 cans chili beans
1 can black beans
I can kidney beans
1 dark chocolate bar
Half can corn
Splash of black coffee
Various spices

Preparation:
Cook all meat together; add 1/4 cup brown sugar and tablespoon paprika when it starts to brown.
Cook onions with butter and teaspoon of paprika and tablespoon of brown sugar.
When onions are see-through add to meat with a quick drizzle of maple syrup. Add veggies and beans and chocolate.
Sprinkle chili pepper, onion powder and garlic to taste.
Let cook on low heat.
An hour before serving, spice to taste.

Clarissa's Lentil (or Split Pea) Soup
Claire Kendal

"...they mocked her and emptied her peas and lentils into the ashes, so that she was forced to sit and pick them out again."
"Cinderella", The Brothers Grimm

 Lentils and peas are the stuff of fairy tales, which is why Clarissa cooks this soup in The Book of You. Although the soup—and a number of other things—don't turn out quite as Clarissa would wish, this recipe is easy to make and one of my favourite things to eat.
 The soup needs a full day of cooking time. It's best to prepare it in the morning so it can then simmer all day. You need a huge soup pan with a well-fitting lid, so use the biggest one you have (my favourite is a deep, cauldron-sized, cast-iron and enamel-lined casserole).
 This recipe makes 6-8 large servings, depending on the size of the bowls you use. It's also a lovely thing to make for fewer people, so that there will be some to reheat and eat the next day.

 Ingredients:
- 6 large, strong onions
- 8-10 medium/large carrots (around a kilogram, or 2 pounds)
- 8-10 sticks of celery (about 450 grams, or 15-16 ounces)
- 500 grams (16-17 ounces) fresh spinach, washed
- Vegetable oil
- Vegetable stock powder (my favourite is Marigold Swiss Vegetable Bouillon, but you can use whatever kind you like best)
- Hot chili powder

500 grams, or 16-17 ounces, of dried lentils or dried split peas. Any colour of lentils (green, red or yellow) or split peas (green or yellow) will work, depending on your preference or what is in your cupboard.

Preparation:
The night before...
The night before you plan to cook the soup, put the lentils (or split peas) to soak in a large bowl. Cover them with plenty of water, and mix 1 teaspoon of stock powder and 1 teaspoon of chili powder i
nto the liquid (this may sound like an odd thing to do, but I think it mysteriously helps). Cover the bowl and leave them in the seasoned water overnight. They should be hugely swollen the next morning, with most of the fluid absorbed.

The next morning... Making the soup...
Wash the celery, then chop it into large chunks. Peel and roughly chop the onions. Put the celery and onions into the cauldron-sized soup pan with 4 tablespoons of vegetable oil, a tablespoon of stock powder, and 3 teaspoons of chili powder (don't worry that it will be too spicy—the seasonings will lose strength during cooking, and be absorbed by the other things you will add). Stir these ingredients well, then cover and cook gently for about half an hour, until the vegetables are softened and reduced a bit in volume.

While the onions and celery are softening, do the following four things. Periodically check the onions and celery, stirring them and adjusting the heat to make sure they don't burn or stick to the bottom. Put a large kettle or pan of water to boil. Peel and chop the carrots into half-inch thick round slices. Thoroughly rinse the lentils or split peas, checking that there aren't any bits of grit or small stones in them.

Add the carrots and lentils (or split peas) to the cauldron containing the now-softened and reduced vegetables. Pour in the boiling water, stopping about two inches from the top of the cauldron so the liquid doesn't spill over while cooking and make a mess (don't ask me how I know this). Add more stock powder (about 4 teaspoons) plus an additional teaspoon of chili powder. Once the mixture starts to bubble gently, put the washed spinach on top until it wilts. You want the spinach to shrink dramatically in volume so that it can then be mixed in without making everything overflow. Once the spinach has shrunk, stir it in—it will disappear quickly.

Cover the soup and let it gently bubble all day, checking every hour and stirring. Add more boiling water from the kettle if too much fluid has evaporated—you want the soup to stay about two inches from top of the cauldron. The longer you give this soup to cook, the better it tastes.

A couple of hours before eating, check the seasoning and add an extra teaspoon or two of stock powder if needed, and/or an extra sprinkle of chili powder—you want to do this while there is still some cooking time left, so that the additional seasoning can meld into the soup. The stock powder I use contains salt, so I don't need to put any more in; but if this isn't the case with your brand, add salt to taste.

Once the soup is ready, I do one of three things.

The first option is serve the soup as it is—a kind of thick broth full of chunks of vegetables.

The second option is to blend the soup, and it's lovely this way too, but quite different. Because the cauldron will be too heavy and too dangerously full of hot liquid to risk moving it, I let the soup cool a bit. Then I bring the blender jug over to the oven as well as an empty (and very large) saucepan. I decant the soup from the cauldron into the blender with a ladle. I blend about a pint at a time, transferring each blended pint into the new saucepan. I repeat this process until all of the soup is blended and the original cauldron is empty.

The third option (which is what I most often do) is to blend some and leave some, so I can eat it in one form that night and in the other form the next day. This option also pleases my daughters, who are strongly divided in their views about the ideal consistency of soup.

Claire Kendal is the author of The Book of You.

Big Johnson's White Chili
Matthew McBride

Do you love chili? Of course you do. Everybody loves chili. Out here in the country, we really love it. Chili is important. I even wrote a scene in my book where my protagonist eats a bowl of chili at a strip club (no, really. I did). That's how much I love chili. So a few years back, after several cold beers and many shots of tequila, I managed to talk my buddy, Big Johnson—famous for hoarding his recipes—out of this recipe for white chili.

What's white chili?

Ingredients:
    1 clove garlic, minced
    1 medium onion, diced (1 cup to a cup and a half)
    2 teaspoons of ground cumin (recipe calls for 1 teaspoon, but I love my chili hot. Cumin is hot)
    1 tablespoon of olive oil
    2 stalks celery, diced
    4 cups of chicken broth
    3/4 tablespoon dried oregano
    2 cans of white beans (I like Great Northern)
    3 medium poblano* peppers / gut the seeds and carve out the white ribs
    1/2 teaspoon of cayenne* pepper
    Half a bag** of chicken breasts

* As previously stated, I love my chili HOT. Damn hot. We have our own pepper garden; so if you wish to test the limits of human endurance, I suggest habanero's.

** You can adjust this ratio but I like a lot of chicken in my white chili.

Directions:
Heat the oil in a large pot / medium

Add onion, celery, and poblano peppers. Cook about ten minutes, stirring occasionally.

Add the cumin and the garlic and the other spices. Let simmer and cook. Stir.

Add chicken and white beans and broth and oregano. Cook partially covered. Stir.

Add more pepper and more spices. Whatever you want to throw in there.

Disclaimer: Some recipes actually suggest that you mix yogurt in with the chili. But let me tell you something: here at Crimespree we take our chili seriously. Chili is powerful and manly and eaten by men with mustaches. Yogurt has no business in the same meal as white chili.

Matthew McBride is the author of Frank Sinatra in a Blender *(New Pulp Press). He lives on a farm outside Mount Sterling, Missouri. He has two kids, three dogs, a cat, and a bull. When he's not writing books or causing trouble, he's eating chili.*

Soupe à l'Oignon
M.J. Rose

One of the great influences in my life was my great-grandmother, Annie Berger, who came from a long line of Jewish Gypsies.

From her mother she learned how to sew and how to use a crystal ball to tell the fortunes of her friends and family and how to cook.

Ingredients:
- 1 onion for every person
- 1 knob of butter for every onion
- 1 cup of good beef broth for every knob of butter
- 1 cup of wine
- Salt and pepper

Preparation:
Cut the onions in quarters. Caramelize them in the butter until they are golden. Add the wine and the broth and simmer for 1 hour.

Slice stale bread, butter it, add slices of Gruyere cheese on top and toast till melted. Add two slices to every bowl of soup.

Thai Chicken and Coconut Soup
Kieran Shea

Ingredients:
- 1 lemongrass stalk (sliced)*
- 1/2 tablespoon galangal (grated...if you can't find, fresh ginger works too)*
- 2 lime leafs (torn)*
- 1 shallot (peeled, sliced thin)
- 1 clove of garlic (peeled, sliced)
- 2 skinless organic chicken breasts (diced)
- 2 cups of de-stemmed, Shiitake mushroom caps (sliced into strips)
- 1/2 a fresh lemon
- 1/4 cup of chopped cilantro leaves
- 1 jalapeno pepper (sliced, with seeds)
- 1 very small Thai pepper (seeded and chopped fine)*
- 1 cup of coconut milk
- 40 ounces of quality chicken stock
- Butter
- Salt and freshly ground pepper
- Sugar

Method:

In a stock pot, get your chicken stock going over medium high heat and reduce it a bit to intensify the flavor. You can use chicken broth, but a good stock (the fond de cuisine as the French say) adds a depth of flavor and soul. Toss in the torn lime leaf, sliced lemongrass, sliced garlic, grated galangal into the stock and let the flavors simmer for a bit, maybe twenty minutes or so. Yin a way, you're making a tea and you want to taste the added ingredients. Steep too long and you'll know when you've screwed it up.

Meanwhile, season the shiitakes slices with a little salt and freshly ground pepper and sauté them in a frying pan with smidge of butter. When the mushrooms start to release their liquid, squeeze a little lemon juice over them and remove the mushrooms from heat. Do not drain the mushrooms or I swear to God I will track you down and beat you around the head and neck.

Now then, using a screen strainer, transfer the flavored stock to a good sized sauce pot or second stock pot and bring the strained stock back to a simmer. Trust me, nobody wants to eat lemongrass or torn lime leaf...so straining is a pretty good idea. Discard the strained ingredients. Add the chicken to the now much more flavorful, simmering stock. When the chicken is just about poached, add the coconut milk, the mushrooms with their liquid, a nice pinch of sugar, another squeeze of lemon juice, the sliced shallots, a few jalapeno slices, the cilantro, and the finely diced Thai pepper to the stock. Serve piping hot and bask in your guests' awe. (4 servings)

SALADS

"As I see it, a green salad is an open invitation to carrots, onions, mushrooms, tomatoes, and the sprouts that grow in jars on my kitchen counter."
—Victoria Moran

Summer Cilantro Pasta Salad
Ellie Alexander

Ingredients:
- 2 tablespoons butter
- 1 small onion, minced
- 3 medium tomatoes, chopped to 1/2-inch dice
- 1 1/2 cups chicken stock
- 2 pre-cooked chicken breasts, chopped
- 2 ears of fresh corn, shucked and kernels stripped, or 1 (11 ounces) box of frozen corn
- 2 tablespoons cornstarch
- 2 tablespoons water
- 1/2 bunch of cilantro, chopped
- 2 tablespoons cream
- 1 box Angel Hair pasta, cooked al dente

Directions:
Melt butter over medium heat in a large frying pan. Sauté onions for five minutes, or until translucent. Add tomatoes and sauté for five more minutes. Add chicken stock, bring to a boil. When boiling, add chopped chicken and corn. Reduce heat and simmer for five minutes or until ready to serve. Just before serving mix cornstarch and water in a separate container. Add to sauce to thicken. Stir in cilantro and cream. Serve over angel hair pasta. Delicious served hot or cold.

Soprano Salad
Anonymous-9

Love salad? Are you better with a Mossberg than a melon baller? This dressed-up salad with a citrus twist is so easy any mook could toss it. Add shrimp or chicken to make a main course for two people. Double recipe to serve four.

Ingredients:
- 1 large cooked beet
- 1 juicy orange
- Zesty Italian dressing to taste
- 1/3 bag washed arugula
- 1/2 bag romaine lettuce
- 3 ounces shredded mozzarella cheese

Directions:
Cut beet into slim wedges.
Peel and prepare orange, separating into segments.
Toss romaine and arugula with Italian dressing.
Divide the greens among 2 plates.
Top with beet wedges, orange segments, mozzarella. Serve.

Anonymous-9 is the author of the Hard Bite series, published by Blasted Heath, New Pulp Press, and Down & Out Books.

Lemon Vinaigrette on Greens
Kristi Belcamino

Mix following ingredients in a jar and shake. Serve over four cups torn Romaine lettuce:

Ingredients:
- 1/4 cup lemon juice
- 1/4 cup vegetable oil
- 1/4 cup olive oil
- 2 green onions, finely chopped
- 1 tablespoon minced fresh Italian parsley
- 1 1/2 teaspoons sugar
- 1/2 teaspoon ground mustard
- 1/4 teaspoon salt and 1/8 teaspoon pepper

Spicy Peanut Noodle Salad
Libby Fischer Hellman

Spicy Dressing:
    1/4 cup creamy peanut butter
    1/4 cup soy sauce
    1/ 4 cup peanut oil
    1/4 cup water
    3 tablespoons fresh lemon juice
    3 tablespoons brown sugar
    1 large clove of fresh garlic pressed (You can use more)
    1/2 teaspoons cayenne pepper

Put all these ingredients into a blender until well mixed. Set aside or refrigerate until salad is assembled.

Salad:
    1 package fresh linguine
    1/2 cup fresh bean sprouts
    1 bunch green onions cut into small pieces
    Radishes (maybe 7-10) shredded or minced fine
    1 jar of dry roasted peanuts

Boil salted water and cook fresh linguine. When done, rinse and cut with kitchen shears into 3-inch lengths into a big bowl.

To the pasta add: cut up green onions, bean sprouts, and shredded radishes. When this is all in your bowl, add reserved dressing and toss. Refrigerate until serving time. Add the peanuts just before serving. DO NOT MAKE THIS THE DAY BEFORE—the bean sprouts will not be crunchy.

You can add other ingredients if you wish, e.g. shrimp, chicken or even pork.

Wild Rice and Cranberry Salad
John Lutz

Ingredients:
- 1 6-ounce package. long grain and wild rice (Uncle Ben's either reg. or instant)
- 1 cup sweetened dried cranberries
- 1 cup fresh broccoli flowerets chopped
- 4 green onions chopped
- 3 celery ribs thinly sliced
- 1 2-ounce jar pimentos sliced and drained
- 1 cup sweet and sour dressing (1/2 cup each of sugar, vinegar and oil, blended in blender)
- 1 cup dry roasted peanuts

Preparation:
Prepare rice according to package directions. Cool. Combine rice with the next five ingredients.
  Add dressing. Stir gently. Cover and chill overnight or at least two hours. Stir in peanuts just before serving. Serves 6-8

Red Bean Salad
John Lutz

A bean salad that my mother made and was on the Sunday dinner table nearly every week while I was growing up

Ingredients:
- 1 can red beans drained (not the lg. kidney beans)
- 1 hard-boiled egg, chopped
- 1 teaspoons pickle relish
- 2 stalks celery, chopped
- Miracle Whip to taste

Mix, chill. Serves 4-6

Strawberry Salad
Penny Halle

Salad:
- 1 bunch of baby spinach
- 1 head of red lettuce
- 2 pints of sliced strawberries
- 1 cup chopped roasted pecans

To roast pecans: put pecans on a jelly roll pan with 2 tablespoons butter for ten to twelve minutes stir occasionally.

Dressing:
- 1/3 cup red wine vinegar
- 1 teaspoons salt
- 1/2 cup sugar
- 1 teaspoons dry mustard
- 1-2 tablespoons chopped green onions
- 1 cup salad oil
- 1 tablespoons poppy seed

Works best to shake in a glass jar with a tight lid. Dress the salad just before serving.

Marty Westerfield's Caesar Salad
Boyd Morrison

Ingredients:
    2 tablespoons olive oil
    1 tablespoon balsamic vinegar
    1-2 cloves crushed garlic
    1 head romaine lettuce
    1 raw egg
    3 tablespoons lemon juice
    3/4 teaspoons salt
    Fresh ground pepper
    1/2 cup parmesan, finely grated
    1/4 cup Italian breadcrumbs

Instructions:
Combine oil and vinegar; add crushed garlic and let stand 1 to 2 hours.
    Wash lettuce and dry; break into bite-sized pieces in a large salad bowl.
    Sprinkle with oil/vinegar mixture and toss until greens are glistening.
    Beat egg with fork; add lemon juice, salt, and pepper; mix.
    Pour egg mixture onto lettuce and toss until greens are fully coated.
    Sprinkle with parmesan and breadcrumbs; toss thoroughly.
    Serve immediately.

Nectarine (or peach), Mixed Leaves And Blue Cheese Salad
Ayo Onatade

I am not one of those people that won't eat a salad if it has fruit in it. There is something to be said for having fruit in a salad as it can sometimes offset the tartness of a salad dressing.

The following recipe can be adapted to use different fruit but this is the recipe I generally make the most. It is lovely during the summer and also makes a brilliant starter. Serves 4

Ingredients:
- Mixed salad leaves to include rocket (arugula) enough for 4 people
- 4 ripe nectarines or peaches, halved, pitted and cut into eighths saving any juice and sprinkle with lemon juice to prevent discolouring
- 1 heaped tablespoon pine kernel nuts lightly roasted in a dry frying pan.
- 4 salmon filets (optional)
- Blue Cheese crumbled
- Lemon juice

For the dressing:
- 1 tablespoon honey
- 1 teaspoon wholegrain mustard
- 1 1/2 tablespoons Extra Virgin Olive Oil
- A pinch of salt

For the marinade:
- Light soy sauce
- Black pepper
- Lemon Juice
- Garlic

Preparation:
If you are going to have salmon with the salad to make it a more fulfilling meal then you need to marinade the salmon beforehand.

Mix together the ingredients for the marinade in a bowl and immerse the salmon filets in the marinade cover and leave for thirty minutes at least.

Pre-heat grill for medium heat

Roast the pine kernels in a dry frying pan until lightly brown. Set aside to cool.

Lightly oil grill grate. Place salmon on the preheated grill, and discard marinade. Cook salmon for six to eight minutes per side, or until the fish flakes easily with a fork.

Mix together the ingredients for the salad dressing whisking in the oil until combined adding any juice from the nectarines that you might have saved.

In a bowl toss together the salad leaves, the nectarines and the pine kernels.

Just before serving toss the salad with the dressing.

Share the salad on to four plates sprinkling the crumbled blue cheese on top and serve with the salmon.

Tips:
The other fruit that you can make this with include strawberries or seedless grapes as they work best. If you use strawberries then toss them in some lemon juice and black pepper.

If you want you can also add chopped avocado as well but remember to sprinkle the avocado with some lemon juice to stop it from discolouring.

If you don't want to use salmon then substitute it with trout (which is much lighter), cooked tiger prawns, or Prosciutto.

You can also substitute the blue cheese with torn buffalo mozzarella.

SIDE DISHES

"Sorry, I thought you were done so I ate the rest"
—Jon Jordan

Five Cheese Mac and Cheese
Avery Aames

Ingredients:
- 2 cups dried macaroni, cooked to tender (about 4-5 cups cooked)
- 3 cloves garlic chopped
- 8 tablespoons butter (a cube)
- 1 1/2 cup milk
- 1/2 cup white wine
- 3 Tablespoons rice flour
- 1 teaspoons salt
- 1/2 teaspoons pepper
- 1/2 teaspoons paprika
- 2 cups grated cheese (equal parts Cheddars, Smoked Gouda, Parmesan, Monterey Jack, Havarti)

Directions:

Cook macaroni according to package directions. Drain and set aside. May be made a day ahead. Note: Do not forget to drain and set aside. You do not want the pasta to be "wet."

In a large sauce pan, melt butter over medium heat. Add garlic and cook about 2 minutes. Add rice flour and stir. Cook 1 minute, let boil and thicken, stirring constantly.

Add milk and wine, stir and let boil to thicken.

Remove from heat and add cheeses and seasonings.

Pour sauce over drained macaroni.

Serve with a crisp salad.

Avery Aames is the pseudonym for author Daryl Wood Gerber. Avery writes A Cheese Shop Mystery series. The first, The Long Quiche Goodbye, *is a national bestseller and winner of the Agatha Award for Best First Novel. The second book is* Lost and Fondue. *Avery blogs at Mystery Lovers Kitchen, http://www.mysteryloverskitchen.com/, a blog for foodies who love mysteries.*

Caramelized Brussel Sprouts with Bacon
Maegan Beaumont

Ingredients:
- 2 pounds Brussel sprouts—trimmed and cut in half (quarters if they're big)
- 1 medium white onion—diced
- 2-3 shallot cloves—diced
- 1/2 bacon—cut into small, bite-sized pieces
- 1/2 cup chicken broth
- 1 teaspoons kosher salt
- 1/2 tablespoons. garlic powder

Preparation:
Cook bacon in large skillet at medium high heat, letting it brown before adding onions and shallots. Once bacon is crisp and the onions and shallots are translucent, add Brussel sprouts, giving them a good toss to mix them in with the bacon mixture in the pan. Let them sit cook for a few minutes, stirring occasionally to ensure that all sides of your sprouts are browning evenly—about five to seven minutes. When your sprouts and onions are golden brown, add in your chicken broth and seasoning, giving them another quick stir to deglaze the pan before covering. Let cook for another five minutes or until the Brussel sprouts are tender. Re-season to taste if necessary. Serves 6.

Lemon Vinaigrette on Greens
Kristi Belcamino

Mix following ingredients in a jar and shake. Serve over four cups torn Romaine lettuce:

Ingredients:
- 1/4 cup lemon juice
- 1/4 cup vegetable oil
- 1/4 cup olive oil
- 2 green onions, finely chopped
- 1 tablespoon minced fresh Italian parsley
- 1 1/2 teaspoons sugar
- 1/2 teaspoon ground mustard
- 1/4 teaspoon salt
- 1/8 teaspoon pepper

Cranberry Relish THE BEST!
Robin Burcell

I love cranberries. And anything that includes them are something I gravitate toward!

Here are two cranberry recipes perfect for approaching holiday events:

Cranberry Relish (AKA cranberry sauce that includes real fruit) and Cranberry Freeze Cocktail, the perfect slushy alcoholic drink to serve before or after that party!

Ingredients:
- 12 ounces bag fresh cranberries
- 1 large apple, peeled, cored, chopped coarse. (Granny Smith are great!)
- 1 cup dried golden raisins
- 3/4 cup sugar
- 1/2 cup orange juice
- 1/2 teaspoons cinnamon or ginger
- 1 teaspoons balsamic vinegar—reserve for finishing (for me optional)

Preparation:

Put all the ingredients except vinegar into heavy-bottomed saucepan and stir to combine.

Med. heat. Stirring, bring ingredients to boil.

Lower heat and simmer gently until relish thickens, about five minutes.

Remove from heat. If you prefer a relish, stir in vinegar. If you prefer more of a traditional tasting cranberry sauce, don't add vinegar.

Spoon into heatproof container, cover and cool to room temperature.

Refrigerate. Will keep for two weeks.

Cranberry Freeze Cocktail
Robin Burcell

Ingredients:
- 32 ounces cranberry juice
- 1 large can frozen pink lemonade (Can thaw on countertop for a bit).
- 1 liter ginger ale
- 1-2 cups of whiskey (taste test for preference before adding full 2 cups!)

Preparation:
Mix all ingredients in a large bowl, stir until lemonade is melted. Pour into freezer proof container with lid. Freeze overnight.

Warning! Make sure to leave room for expansion—I speak from experience! Use a large spoon to scrape slush into cups once frozen.

The Wonderful Fruit
Bill Cameron

You don't have to be a fan of Blazing Saddles to be a fan of baked beans. You simply have to love goodness and wonder and delight. Though the original recipe starts with bacon, I have enough vegetarian and vegan friends that I've worked out a delicious vegan variation.

I use a Dutch oven, but the recipe also works in a slow cooker. You can also safely double the recipe for a big crowd, though you won't need quite double the liquid. Cooking time is 6-8 hours, so plan accordingly.

The night before:
1 pound dried Great Northern beans

Soak beans in a covered bowl overnight in enough cold water to submerge them completely, about 6-8 cups.

Bean day:
- 1 pound bacon, chopped (I like to use dry-cured bacon, but any kind works)
- Vegan Variation: enough olive oil to cook the onions at the beginning, about 2-3 tablespoons
- 1 medium yellow onion, chopped
- 2 jalapeños, chopped (Optional) (But, seriously, add jalapeños.)
- 3-5 cloves garlic, chopped fine
- 1 small can tomato paste (Unrelated: sometimes I will sometimes eat tomato paste straight up.)
- 1/4 cup dark brown sugar
- 1/4 cup molasses (I have seen recipes which double the brown sugar and skip the molasses. Madness! Do not skip the molasses.)

Vegan Variation: add about 3 tablespoons soy sauce for umami
4 cups liquid: vegetable (vegan) or chicken broth, or reserved water from soaked beans
A pint of stout for half the liquid is also excellent
1/4-1/2 teaspoon cayenne pepper (Or more.)
1/2 teaspoon ground coriander
A hefty dose of fresh ground black pepper (say, a teaspoon or so)
1 teaspoon coarse salt (Smoked salt is excellent if you have it.)
Vegan Variation: add an extra teaspoon salt

Preparation:
Heat oven to 250 degrees F.

Place a cast iron Dutch oven over medium heat and stir in 3/4s of the bacon (or olive oil), onion, and jalapeños until the onions are soft, about five minutes. Add garlic and stir until the flavor opens up, about 1 minute. Stir in the tomato paste, dark brown sugar, and molasses (and soy sauce).

Drain the beans and reserve the soaking liquid. Add the drained beans to the Dutch oven. Add 4 cups liquid. Bring to a boil over high heat. Add in cayenne, coriander, black pepper and salt. (Adjust cayenne to your personal heat preference. I like a little more zing, but even a bare hint is enough.) Give them a stir and cover. Place the Dutch oven in the oven for six to eight hours, or until the beans are tender.

Shortly before serving, cook the remaining chopped bacon until crisp. Garnish the finished beans with the bacon crumblies.

In the need of desperation, we've sampled the beans after four hours. They're good, but if you can give them that extra two to four hours, they're even better. You can also cook them overnight, but if they're going to be in the oven longer than eight hours, drop the oven temp to 225 degrees F so they don't overcook.

We eat them as is, or with a small dollop of sour cream or a little grated cheddar. This is my variation of a recipe I originally saw on Alton Brown. (Beano is optional).

Enjoy!

Myron's Potato Latkes (Pancakes)
Harlan Coben

Ingredients:
- 6 Medium to large potatoes
- 1 large onion (Vidalia preferably)
- 5 tablespoons flour
- 2 Eggs
- 1 teaspoon salt
- 1/2 teaspoon ground red pepper (cayenne)
- Ground black paper to taste
- Vegetable oil (to cover bottom of frying pan 1/4-inch)

Preparation:
Great the potatoes (no need to peel) with a mandolin (preferable) or food processor. Try to make the grating as close to shoestrings as possible for the best texture. Boil the grated potatoes in water for four minutes. Strain and squeeze dry. Mix in all other ingredients (except veg oil).

Form the latkes with your hands—do this by making approximately 3-inch diameter pancakes and flattening them between the palms of your hands to squeeze out the extra liquid. Place in a frying pan with the hot veg oil. When golden brown/crispy, flip them over and repeat on other side. Remove the potato latkes and pat them between paper towels.

Best if served immediately, but they can be kept warm in an oven. Make sure you have plenty of sour cream and applesauce to accompany. Myron like them with Yoo Hoo.

Yield 20-25 latkes.

Lentils and Brown Rice
Alison Dasho

Here's my lentils and brown rice recipe:
- Can of lentils, or two cups dried and reconstituted, if you're fancy and have lots of time on your hands to be soaking legumes
- Olive oil
- Red wine vinegar
- Onion powder
- Coriander
- Salt
- Pepper
- Brown Rice
- Parmesan cheese or Muenster

Preparation:

I prefer to cook using as few dishes as possible, so I don't really measure stuff (sorry!).

Heat up the olive oil in a shallow pan. Throw in the lentils (if you're using canned, be sure to rinse them, this makes a big difference). Then put in roughly two Alison-sized palmsful of coriander, and one good sprinkle of onion powder, and then some salt and pepper. Then several glugs of red wine vinegar. I love vinegar, I would drink it like juice if that weren't totally weird, so this recipe is basically just an excuse for me to get my vinegar-tang fix. Stir it all up and let it simmer while you cook some brown rice in a small pot.

Once the rice is done, plop the lentils into the pot, add either parmesan cheese or some grated Muenster, grab a fork, and enjoy

Alison Dasho enjoys books, knitting, and singing songs. You can find her on Twitter at @alisonedits.

Greens & Beans
Alice Loweecey

Ingredients:
- 2 large bunches endive or all the dandelions from the lawn and garden, if you don't use chemicals on it
- 2 cloves garlic or powdered garlic to taste
- 1 can cannellini beans
- Oil
- Salt and pepper to taste

Preparation:

Boil endive/dandelions in large pot of salted water till done; drain. Slightly crush the garlic and rub around inside of large pot. Then dice garlic, add a bit of oil and fry the garlic in the same pot. (If using powdered garlic, just add it in with the beans.) Add greens, undrained can of beans and 1 can water. Bring to boil, then simmer for fifteen minutes.

Really chewy Italian bread goes best with this.

Red Beans & Rice
Bryan VanMeter

Ingredients:
- 1 pound smoked sausage cut into 1/2-inch pieces. Andouille if you can find a good supply
- 1 large onion diced
- 1 bell pepper diced
- 1 chopped garlic clove
- 1 stalk of celery diced
- 1 pound red beans soaked overnight
- 10 cups of water
- Salt
- 2 tablespoons essence of Emeril

Preparation:
1. Brown sausage and set aside
2. Add onion, celery, and garlic to the pot and cook for seven minutes stirring occasionally
3. Add water, salt, beans, and seasoning. Boil gently for two hours
4. Add sausage and serve over white rice. Feel free to add as much hot sauce as you like.

Purple Hull Pea Recipe
Steve Weddle

Ingredients:
   Small piece salt pork
   4-5 cups shelled and rinsed purple hull peas
   Salt and pepper to taste
   Enough water to cover with an inch on top

Preparation:
Boil salt pork five minutes to remove excess salt. Remove from pan and discard water. Cool slightly then cube salt pork. Place into heavy sauce pan with 2 tablespoons lard (or vegetable oil). Brown. Put peas into sauce pan with browned salt pork. Cover with enough water to have an inch or 2 above peas. Bring to a boil and reduce heat to maintain a gentle boil. Add salt and pepper to taste. Cook until peas are soft, 1 1/2 to 2 hours. Mash a couple of peas in a spoon; taste and adjust for seasoning.)
Serve with hot corn bread.

Optional variations:
Small pods of okra may be cooked in peas.
Chopped onion and/or a couple of garlic cloves may be browned with the salt pork to cook in peas.
If there is no salt pork, cook with a smoked ham hock or a cup of good quality smoked ham, cubed, or a drop or two of liquid smoke.

ENTREES

"Sitting down and sharing a meal together combines two of my favorite loves: eating great food and talking about great food."
—Homaro Cantu

Goat Cheese Fondue
Regular or gluten-free
Avery Aames

Ingredients:
- 3/4 cup cream
- 8 ounces feta cheese
- 1 tablespoon white pepper
- 1 tablespoon green onion (green tips only)
- 1 tablespoon white wine
- 2 teaspoons flour OR 2 teaspoons tapioca flour (for gluten-free)
- 1 baguette bread OR 20-30 gluten-free crackers
- Broccoli florets, steamed
- Carrots, sliced raw
- Celery, sliced raw

Preparation (serves 4):

Warm the cream in a pot until hot but not burning. Use low heat. Add the goat cheese in chunks.

Stir with a whisk to prevent clotting. Add the pepper, wine, green onion tips, and flour/gluten-free flour. Stir approximately five to seven minutes until as smooth as it can be.

Set up your plates with vegetables and bread cubes or crackers. Eat family style.

Note: The thickness of the fondue might vary. If it's too thick, add a little cream. Too thin, add a little more cheese.

Second note: I like to snip the green tips of onions with scissors for even cuts.

Third note: To steam broccoli, perfectly every time. Bring to boil 1 cup water in a 6 quart pot with 1/2 teaspoon salt. Add cut up broccoli. Cover. Cook four minutes. Pour off boiling water. Cover again. Let sit for four minutes. Remove lid and rinse broccoli in cold water to stop the cooking process.

Mel's Texas BBQ Mop Sauce
From the Pampered Pets mystery series
Sparkle Abbey

Melinda Langston owns the high-end Bow Wow Boutique. She sells party dresses, crystal collars, designer pet carries, and dog "pawlish" to the elite in Laguna Beach. That is when she's not busy solving a murder. Though she loves southern California, she hails from the great state of Texas and shares her Lone Star heritage with her friends via her very own sweet and spicy Texas BBQ sauce. Here's Mel's recipe:

You'll need:
 1/4 cup butter
 2 cloves garlic, minced
 1/4 cup minced onion
 3 stalks of celery, chopped
 1 cup water
 1 beef bouillon cube
 1 cup ketchup
 1/2 cup cider vinegar
 3 tablespoons Worcestershire sauce
 2 tablespoons spicy mustard
 2 tablespoons honey
 1 tablespoon paprika
 2 teaspoons chili powder

Preparation:
In a medium sauce pan melt the butter and then add the garlic, onion, and chopped celery. Sauté them until they are lightly browned. Next add the water and bouillon and stir until the cube is dissolved.

Add the rest of the ingredients and stir. Let simmer for at least fifteen minutes. This makes about 3 1/2 cups of sauce. The sauce can be used on beef brisket, pulled pork, or whatever you like. Mel mostly uses it as a mop sauce which means she brushes it on the surface of the meat like a basting sauce during cooking.

Sparkle Abbey is the pseudonym of mystery authors Mary Lee Woods and Anita Carter. They write the national bestselling pet mystery series which features two feuding cousins who solve whodunits set in the wacky world of pampered pets, precious pedigrees, and secrets. The two authors chose to use Sparkle Abbey as their pen name because it combines the names of their two rescue pets, Sparkle (Mary Lee's cat) and Abbey (Anita's dog). Website: http://www.sparkleabbey.com/.

Low-Country Boil
Victoria Allman

This is the easiest recipe for a crowd. Everything is boiled in one pot and ready to eat. There are many brands of spice mix to use: Old Savannah Crab and Shrimp Boil, McCormick's, Old Bay, and Zatarain's Crab and Shrimp Boil. Don't be afraid to leave the shells on the shrimp. Peeling them is half the fun. Make sure to put dishes out to collect the shells or place extra newspaper on the table to wrap up the remains afterwards. The condiment to serve this with is cocktail sauce for dipping.

Ingredients:
- 2 lemons
- 3 liters water
- 1/2 cup spice mix (see above)
- 2 tablespoons sea salt
- 2 white onions, chopped in 1-inch dice
- 2 pounds baby potatoes
- 4 ears of corn, cut in thirds
- 2 pounds kielbasa sausage, cut in 2-inch lengths
- 3 pounds medium-sized shrimp, head off, shell on

Cocktail Sauce:
- 1/4 cup horseradish
- 3/4 cup ketchup
- 2 tablespoons mayonnaise
- 1 tablespoon Dijon mustard
- 2 tablespoons Worcestershire sauce

Preparation:
In a large pot bring water, lemons, onions, potatoes, sea salt, and spice mix to a boil. Simmer for ten minutes. Add sausage

and corn and simmer another seven minutes. Add the shrimp and bring back to a boil. Strain.

Mix ingredients for cocktail sauce and serve on the side for dipping.

Serve with lots of bread and cold beer.

Serves 6

Victoria Allman, author of Sea Stories of Strong Women. *http://www.victoriaallman.com/*

Stealthy Burgers
Anonymous-9

Sneak green veggies inside your burgers and they'll never know how healthy they are!

Ingredients:
  1 1/2 pounds 80/20 ground beef sirloin
  1/3 cup finely chopped flat-leaf parsley (big handful)
  1/3 cup chopped chives (or omit and increase the onion)
  1/3 cup coarse chopped yellow onion
  1 tablespoon Worcestershire sauce (couple good squirts)
  Salt and pepper
  2 tablespoons dijon mustard (or any fancy mustard)
  4 crusty kaiser rolls, split (wholegrain okay)
  4 leaves green-leaf lettuce
  4 chunky slices red tomato
  American cheese slices if desired

Directions:
Preheat a grill or frying pan to medium-high. In a large bowl, combine the beef, parsley, chives, onion and Worcestershire sauce; season with salt and pepper. Divide the mixture into 4 mounds. Grill four minutes on each side for medium.

Stack bottom of each roll with burger, cheese slice, tomato, and lettuce. Add traditional condiments if desired, but not necessary. Top with remaining bun and serve.

Anonymous-9 is the author of the Hard Bite series, published by Blasted Heath, New Pulp Press, and Down & Out Books.

Peposo
Brian Azzarello

This is an old Italian recipe—Renaissance old. The masons who fired the tiles for Brunelleschi's Doumo in Florence originated it and would prepare it in the tile kilns while they were working. This dates it at 1436. That's cool to me, and just adds an extra bite to an incredibly earthy dish that's cooked low and slow.

One of the things that I usually enjoy about cooking is the history—recreating moments from the past—usually handed down from Aunt Lou, my Godmother and the Matron saint of my kitchen. This one speaks to that tradition. Uncle Elmer was a brick layer.

Ingredients:
   2 pounds beef stew meat
   10 cloves of garlic, peeled and left whole
   AT LEAST 2 heaping tablespoons. Cracked (not ground) black pepper
   2 bottles of Chianti (1 for cooking, 1 for while eating)
   A couple sprigs of fresh Rosemary
   A couple bay leaves
   Salt, to taste

Preparation:
Put all ingredients except the salt in a heavy stew pot then pour in enough wine to cover it all. Put lid on pot and stick in an oven pre-heated to 225 degrees. Now go about your business while it cooks for eight hours (or more) very gently, so that the liquid in the pot just barley simmers. While it cooks your place is going to smell great, trust me. Check it occasionally—if liquid starts to boil away add a bit more wine and turn down heat. Don't worry, it will be fine. At the end of the cooking time

remove rosemary twigs and bay leaves. Take a fork to it; the meat should fall apart, mingling with liquid and creating a rich gravy. The garlic will have dissolved, but if not bust it up too. Add salt to taste.

Serve over crusty toasted bread rubbed with garlic. Open second bottle of wine and enjoy.

I usually start this about 8 am and let it go all day. Yeah, it takes a long time, but damn if it's not worth it.

Gnocchi with Gorgonzola Sauce
Kristi Belcamino

This recipe was in an early draft of my novel, *Blessed are the Dead*, but that chapter didn't make the final cut. There is a bit of a story behind this sauce.

My brother used to live in the Village in NYC and my husband and I used to go visit him for long weekends and pretend we lived there. We told him, just do what you normally do (we'd been to NYC enough times to hit all the must-see tourist spots and so now we wanted to tour as locals).

My main goal was pretending like I lived there and eating good food.

My brother and I are Italian, so of course we had to hit Little Italy. It was a tough decision choosing which restaurant to eat at, but one maitre'd standing outside convinced us to dine at his establishment. He said, "Call me Uncle Tony" and took us to probably the best table in the place. Then he offered to order for us off the menu. He said the gnocchi with gorgonzola sauce wasn't on the menu, but the cooks always made it special for him and that I should have it. Of course, I agreed.

It was amazing. I asked him for the recipe.

My brother and I were on our second bottle of wine and I wasn't sure I'd remember exactly what he said. I asked my husband, who wasn't drinking if he would remember it for me and he said no problem. My brother said, "Are you sure? Because I can always call my voice mail and leave the recipe there and then we have it for sure." My husband said, "Nah, I got it."

A few weeks later we were back in Minneapolis and I asked my husband what the recipe was for the gorgonzola sauce because I wanted to make it for dinner. Nope. He forgot.

So I called my brother. He didn't remember, either.

A week later, my brother called. "I got somebody who wants to talk to you. Hold on."

Then I heard another voice get on the line, "Hey, it's Uncle Tony."

And he gave me the following recipe:

Ingredients:
- 7 ounces of Gorgonzola cheese crumbles
- 1/3 cup of butter
- 1 1/4 cups of heavy whipping cream
- 1/2 cup of freshly grated Parmigiano
- Salt and pepper to taste
- Package of premade gnocchi

Directions:
1. Heat water for gnocchi.
2. Melt Gorgonzola and butter in a pot over low heat, stirring gently.
3. Once cheese and butter has melted, add whipping cream and cook for a few more minutes until sauce is thick and warmed through. Season with salt and pepper.
4. Meanwhile, drop gnocchi into boiling water. As soon as it floats to the surface it is cooked and can be taken out with a slotted spoon and put into the sauce.
5. Serve with a salad.

Get It Right Grilled Salmon
Lou Berney

I learned this recipe a long ago from a guy I worked with in a restaurant kitchen. The guy was kind of a sociopath (I know, I know, that describes about half the people who work in restaurant kitchens), but/and the guy took his food very seriously. Here's what he told me:

Most important thing, get a good piece of fish, center cut. Don't be an asshole, all right? Go to a fish market, not a grocery store. You can't find a fish market, don't eat fish. Simple as that, it doesn't take a genius.

Heat up your grill. Get it hot. The hotter the better. You want to use a gas grill, that's fine, but I like charcoal better. Either way, get it hot. Did I mention that?

Brush some olive oil on the salmon. Use extra virgin olive, the best you can find. Spend the money—you won't be sorry. The best olive oil in the world comes from Greece. In my opinion. Use high-quality sea salt and fresh-ground pepper. Anything else, you might as well rub that beautiful piece of fish on your ass and stick it in the microwave.

Put the salmon on the grill, flesh side down. Somebody tells you to put the salmon skin side down, that's the kind of person should stick to frozen fish sticks.

Grill the salmon flesh-side down for about eight minutes or so. It depends—how thick is the piece of fish, how hot is the grill? Use your brain. I can't come to your house and hold your hand.

After eight minutes or so, flip the salmon over. Grill it another two or three minutes. Take it off the grill and hit it with some lemon. Hit it was a good lemon. You sensing a theme here yet? I hope so.

That's it. That's all you need. Fish, olive oil, salt, pepper, lemon. If you screw that up, I don't know what to tell you.

Lou Berney is the author of Gutshot Straight, Whiplash River, *and (forthcoming in February of 2015)* The Long and Faraway Gone.

Elk Chili Con Carne
CJ Box

Well, first you need to shoot an elk. Then you can make great chili.
(This recipe was adapted and modified from a Food Network primer.)

Ingredients:
- 6 slices bacon
- 2 pounds chopped elk steaks (round steaks are best)
- 2 large onions, chopped
- 1 large green bell pepper, chopped
- 4 cloves garlic, finely chopped (I use Penzey's)
- Kosher salt
- 1/4 cup chili powder
- 1 tablespoon ground cumin
- 4 teaspoons paprika
- 2 teaspoons dried oregano
- 2 tablespoons tomato paste
- 1 12-ounce bottle amber beer (I like Shiner Bock)
- 2 tablespoons unsweetened cocoa powder
- 1 28-ounce can whole plum tomatoes, crushed by hand
- 1 1/2 cups low-sodium beef broth, plus more if needed
- 2 15-ounce cans black beans, drained and rinsed
- 3 tablespoons hot sauce
- Shredded cheddar cheese, sliced scallions and/or sour cream, for topping (optional)

Preparation:

Cook the bacon in a large saucepan or Dutch oven over medium heat until crisp, 6 to 8 minutes per side. Drain on a paper towel-lined plate and let cool, then crumble and set aside. Pour off all but 1 tablespoon of the bacon drippings from the saucepan (reserve the drippings). Increase the heat to medium high, add the chopped elk and cook, breaking up the meat with a wooden spoon, until browned, about 8 minutes. Transfer to a plate using a slotted spoon; wipe out the pan.

Heat 1 tablespoon of the reserved bacon drippings in the saucepan over medium-high heat. Add the onion and bell pepper and cook, stirring, until soft, about 5 minutes. Add the garlic and 1 teaspoon salt and cook 2 minutes. Add the chili powder, cumin, paprika, oregano and tomato paste and cook, stirring, until the tomato paste is brick red, about 6 minutes (add a splash of water if the mixture begins to stick). Add the beer and simmer until almost completely reduced, about 3 minutes.

Stir in the beef and any juices from the plate; add the cocoa powder, tomatoes, beef broth and beans and bring to a simmer over low heat. Cook, stirring occasionally, until the chili thickens slightly, about 1 hour, 30 minutes.

Stir the hot sauce into the chili and season with salt. Add some beef broth if the chili is too thick. Ladle into bowls and top with the crumbled bacon, cheese, scallions and/or sour cream.

Gutsy Penne 'n Sausage
Rob Brunet

Sometimes when entertaining, you'll want guests to see you knead a little raw meat with your bare hands before wielding a good knife. Call it mood-setting.

Prep time: 30 minutes/Cook time: 30 minutes+

Ingredients:
- 3 tablespoons olive oil
- A few links of fresh Italian sausage (the spicier the better)
- A couple big onions
- 2-3 peppers, any color, sweet or hot, mix and match
- 1 28-ounce can of whole tomatoes (not San Marzano, 'cause this ain't a red sauce)
- 1 pound of penne rigate (or your favourite pasta, but this meal's good for stabbing)
- 1 cup of chopped fresh herbs (basil, parsley, oregano are all good)

Preparation:
In a large saucepan, warm the olive oil over medium heat.

Slice the intestines holding the meat in place, one clean slit lengthwise on each link. Peel the skin back and pinch cherry-sized chunks of meat into the heated oil. It'll sizzle.

While the meat browns, chop the onions, not too fine. Toss 'em in with the meat. Stir it.

Chop the peppers large, like an inch square. Add 'em to the pot once the onions are translucent. Turn the heat to medium low. Stir.

Open the tomatoes and drain the juice into a couple cocktail glasses. (This'd be a good time to improvise Bloody Marys for you and your guests.) Drop the tomatoes in the pot and stir.

Simmer the sauce for at least 30 minutes. An hour or so is better. Break up the tomatoes with a wooden spoon along the way.

Prepare the pasta al dente, strain, and toss it with the sauce, adding the fresh herbs for one final toss before serving.

Broiled Sea Bass with Pineapple-Chili-Basil Glaze
Alafair Burke

Ingredients:
- 3 tablespoons pineapple preserves
- 2 tablespoons rice vinegar
- 1 teaspoon chopped fresh or 1/4 teaspoon dried basil
- 1/8 teaspoon crushed red pepper
- 1 garlic clove, minced
- 3/4 teaspoon salt, divided
- 4 (6-ounce) sea bass or other firm white fish fillets (about 1-inch thick)
- 1/4 teaspoon black pepper
- Cooking spray

Preparation:
1. Preheat broiler.
2. Combine first 5 ingredients and 1/4 teaspoon salt in a small bowl.
3. Sprinkle the fillets with 1/2 teaspoon salt and black pepper.

Place the fillets on a broiler pan coated with cooking spray; broil 5 minutes. Remove from oven; brush fillets evenly with glaze. Return to oven; broil for an additional 5 minutes or until the fish flakes easily when tested with a fork.

Yield: 4 servings (serving size: 1 fillet)

Chili
Dana Cameron

Dana's note: I like this because it's easy, and makes enough for leftovers and freezing. Also, I can't do spicy-hot, but like flavorful food; if you do like hot food, this basic recipe will work well with whatever you add to it. The chocolate gives it a great background flavor and richness. Serve with corn bread, corn chips, or rice.

Ingredients:
- 1 1/2 pounds ground sirloin (or you can use ground or shredded turkey, chicken, pork)
- 4-5 8-ounce cans tomato sauce
- 1 large onion, chopped
- 2 large green peppers, chopped (optional)
- 2 cloves minced garlic (more, if you want)
- 1/4 teaspoons cayenne pepper
- 1 teaspoons celery seed
- 1 1/2 teaspoons cumin
- 1 bay leaf (optional)
- 2 1/2 tablespoons chili powder
- 1/2 teaspoons basil
- Dash of salt
- 1 tablespoons white vinegar
- 1 tablespoons baker's chocolate (semi-sweet is best, but you can use anything less sweet than that)
- 2 15-ounce cans red kidney beans (using half black beans will work, too)

Preparation:
Brown meat. Add rest of the ingredients. Bring to a boil; then reduce heat to low. Simmer for 45 minutes to an hour, at least.

Hot Brown
Christy Campbell

A little back ground on this one... The Hot Brown originated at The Brown Hotel in Louisville, Ky. Growing up in Louisville, I enjoyed this the day after Thanksgiving. Leftover turkey is must and the best way to use those leftovers.

This recipe makes 2 hot browns.

Ingredients:
- 3 tablespoons butter
- 3 tablespoons flour
- 1 1/2 cups heavy cream
- 1/4 cup shredded parmesan cheese
- 1/4 cup sharp cheddar cheese
- Salt and pepper to taste
- 2 cups cooked and sliced turkey
- 4 slices white bread
- 8 slices cooked bacon
- 1 sliced tomato (I like it diced)

Preparation:
In a 2 quart sauce pan melt butter. Slowly mix in flour and make a roux (paste). Cook roux for 2 minutes.

Watch the roux and keep on medium to low heat. Add the cream and bump heat up to medium. Cook for 2 to 3 minutes at which time it should simmer. Take off the heat add parmesan and cheddar cheese. It will melt keep stirring. Add salt and pepper to taste.

In an oven proof dish, add the white bread (which you have toasted). Next add turkey. Follow by the cheesy roux sauce. Tomato slice on top of cheese (It is traditionally done this way. I like it diced). Finally add the 2 slices bacon, crisscrossed on top of tomatoes. Add a pinch of extra parmesan cheese. Place dish in broiler and watch until the cheese melts.

Enjoy!

Noni's Raviolis
My grandmother's famous recipe
Kathryn Casey

Cheese Filling:
- 1 1/4 pounds Havarti (or white brick cheese if you can find it)
- 1 1/4 pounds Muenster
- 1 cup grated Fontinella (can substitute a good Parmesan)
- 3 slightly beaten eggs
- 1/2 cups finely chopped parsley
- Pepper
- Garlic powder to taste
- Parmesan cheese to sprinkle on the top of the casserole

Preparation:
Grate cheeses and mix together. Add eggs plus shake in some pepper and garlic powder, and the parsley. Mix again, then break off small amounts (a tablespoon or so) and roll in your palms to make balls. (makes about 70)

Dough: Double this recipe. Each makes about 1 pound of pasta dough.
- 3.5 cups unbleached, all-purpose flour
- 4 extra-large eggs (allow to warm on counter for a while)
- 1/2 teaspoons extra-virgin olive oil

Preparation:
Mound the flour in the center of a large wooden cutting board. Make a well in the middle of the flour and add the eggs and olive oil. Using a fork, beat together the eggs and oil and begin to incorporate the flour starting with the inner rim of the well.

Keep working in more and more of the flour, but don't break down the walls until the end. When about half the flour is incorporated in with the eggs and oil, it should start coming together. You can then start kneading the dough, working in the remainder of the flour. Throw away the little dry bits that don't work in, then continue to knead the dough for another seven minutes. It should form a ball and start feeling smooth, elastic. When you're done kneading, wrap the ball of dough in plastic wrap and let it sit at room temperature for 30 minutes. (Don't skip this. It's important to let the dough rest.)

You can then either use a pasta machine to roll out and polish the dough or do it with a rolling pin. To do it with a rolling pin, cut off a section of the dough, put on a floured surface. Flour the rolling pin, and roll the section of dough out to desired thinness. (It should be quite thin for ravioli.) Cut into squares large enough to accommodate your cheese balls. Place one cheese ball on each square. Fold the dough square over the cheese and into a triangle. Press the edges together. If the dough doesn't seal dab a little water between the pasta layers. Crimp the edges with a fork.

To freeze ravioli: Place on a towel on a cookie sheet, not touching, cover with a towel (you can do this in layers if you have a lot of raviolis), and put in the freezer. Allow four hours. When raviolis are frozen, put in freezer bags and store in the freezer.

To cook: boil lightly salted water, add ravioli (frozen or fresh, don't overcrowd). Boil in batches until pasta is not quite done. (It's only a couple of minutes. They'll start to swell up and float.) For each batch, remove ravs from water and gently rinse to get rid of some of the starch. Have a lasagna pan ready along with your favorite tomato sauce or marinara and grated Parmesan. As the raviolis are cooked, begin layering the casserole, kind of like lasagna. Start with sauce, then ravs, then sauce and cheese, then ravs. Repeat. End with sauce and top with parmesan cheese sprinkled over the top.

Bake your finished casserole at 350 degrees for approximately 45 minutes, although the exact time will depend on your pan and oven and the size of the casserole. It should be steaming, bubbling around the edges. (We usually pull one from the center to taste to make sure it's done.)

Mom Chandler's Stroganoff
Jesse Chandler

Ingredients:
   2 pounds browned ground beef
   2 cans mushroom soup
   1 package Lipton onion dry soup mix
   1 package dry Hidden Valley buttermilk dressing
   1 package noodles boiled and drained
   1 canned mushrooms, optional
   1 pint/2 cups sour cream

Add all of the ingredients and let simmer for 10 or 15 minutes. Thicken with flour or cornstarch if needed. Serve sauce over noodles or mix together. It's wickedly delish!

Chipotle Chicken Pot Pie
Joelle Charbonneau

The holidays are coming. With them comes colder weather and leftover turkey. Here's a way to add a little heat to your meals while making sure all that turkey doesn't go to waste.

Chipotle chicken pot pie
- 4 tablespoons butter
- 4 tablespoons flour
- 12 ounces chicken broth
- 1 1/2 cups of 2% milk
- 1/2 teaspoon smoked paprika
- 1/2 teaspoon salt
- 1-2 chipotle peppers minced—depends on your spice preference
- 6 cloves of garlic-minced
- 1 medium onion-diced
- 5 carrots-chopped
- 1 cup chopped celery
- 1 red pepper-chopped
- 1 yellow pepper-chopped
- 5 potatoes—peeled and diced into 1-inch pieces
- Leftover turkey or if you don't have turkey left over use 1 Rotisserie chicken (yeah-you can make your own if you really want to, but why?)-chop into 1-inch pieces
- 8 ounces of frozen petit peas
- 1 egg
- 2 tablespoons water

Crust
- 1/2 cup butter
- 2 cups flour
- 1 large sweet potato peeled, boiled and mashed

Preparation:

Cut 1/2 cup butter into flour. Then mix mashed sweet potato into the flour mixture. Once combined, put the dough on wax paper and let it refrigerate for at least an hour.

Melt 4 tablespoons butter in a pan. Add flour and stir while cooking for 2 minutes. Add chicken stock while stirring with a whisk...the sauce will get very thick. Slow whisk in milk. If the sauce is still too thick you can add more milk or chicken stock. Add smoked paprika and salt. Set sauce to the side.

Coat the bottom of a large pan with olive oil. Add onions, carrots and celery. Cook on medium heat for about 5 minutes. Add garlic and chipotle peppers. Stir and cook for 30 seconds before adding bell peppers, chicken and potatoes. Let cook for 5 minutes then combined mixture with sauce. Stir in frozen peas and pour into a large casserole dish.

Roll out sweet potato dough on a large cutting board and place over the top of the mixture. Crimp at the edges. Cut several ventilation holes in the top of the dough. Whisk together egg and water in a bowl and brush on top of the crust.

Bake in pre-heated 375 degree oven for 45- 50 minutes. Serve!

Maque Chou
Sean Chercover

Maque Chou ("mock-shoo") originated with the American Indians of southern Louisiana, who introduced it to the Creoles and Cajuns. Usually a side dish, it can be converted into a main with the addition of a pound of chicken, pork, duck, gator, or crawfish tails. Can be made vegetarian, if that's the way you roll (see modifications below). Quick and easy to make. Delicious.

Here's what you need:
- Enough bacon to make 1/4 cup of drippings (Vegetarians: 1/4 cup peanut oil)
- 2 medium onions, coarsely chopped
- 1 medium green pepper, stemmed and seeded, coarsely chopped
- 2-3 cloves garlic, chopped
- 1/4 cup fresh parsley, finely chopped
- 4 cups frozen corn kernels, thoroughly defrosted
- 1 28-ounce can whole tomatoes, drained and coarsely chopped, liquid reserved (or 2 large fresh tomatoes, but quality canned tomatoes work just fine)
- 1 cup dry white wine (or water, but wine adds nice flavor)
- 1 teaspoons Tabasco (more or less, to taste)
- 2 teaspoons Cajun seasoning (I recommend Andy Roo's or Joe's Stuff, but whatever)
- 1 teaspoons salt, to taste (careful, most Cajun seasoning has a lot of salt, so add that first and taste, salt near the end.
- 1 CD of awesome Louisiana music (Professor Longhair highly recommended)

Here's what you do:
Put the music on the stereo and turn it up loud. Open the wine and drink a glass. Refill glass. Dance around the kitchen. Chop ingredients that need chopping, while drinking wine and singing along with the music.

In a heavy 4-5 quart pot (dutch oven, casserole, whatever) fry the bacon crisp, remove and set aside, leaving oil (Veggies: just heat the peanut oil). Add the onions and cook over medium heat, stirring frequently, until translucent (about 5 minutes). Add garlic and parsley. Stir in the corn, green pepper, tomatoes, tomato liquid, wine, Cajun seasoning and Tabasco. Bring to a boil over high heat. Reduce heat to low, cover the pot partially, and simmer about 15 minutes, stirring occasionally, until corn is tender. Taste and adjust seasoning. Serve immediately.

Options:
1. If you didn't go the Veggie route, you've got a bunch of crisp bacon sitting to the side. Crumble some over the maque chou upon serving. Yummy.

2. If adding meat to make this a main course, simply cut animal of choice into manageable pieces and sauté in an oiled pan with a little extra garlic and Cajun seasoning. Then add to the pot, when adding corn and tomatoes, and cook the dish a little longer. If adding crawfish, no need to sauté first or cook longer—just toss the little critters in and you're good to go.

Serves 4 hungry people, 6 less-hungry people.

Tortilla Casserole
Judy Clemens

This is a great dish for sharing—for a potluck, to take to someone who needs meals brought into their home, for a party—and is fun to eat! Kids love it, and best of all, you don't need silverware!

Ingredients:
- 1 pound ground beef
- 1 onion, chopped
- 6 corn tortillas (soft, not crispy)
- 1 cup sour cream
- 1 can cream of chicken soup
- 1 jar salsa (how hot you want it is up to you)
- 2 cups shredded cheese (I use Mexican mix, but you can use whatever you want)
- Bag of tortilla chips

Preparation:
Brown the beef with the onion. Make sure you drain the icky grease out when you're done.

Mix the sour cream, the soup, and half of the salsa in a separate bowl.

Spread the other half of the salsa on the bottom of a casserole dish. (I use a 9x9 glass dish)

Tear up 3 of the tortillas and layer them on top of the salsa.

Spread half of the meat mixture on top of the torn up tortillas, half of the sour cream mixture on top of the beef, and half of the cheese on top of the sour cream mixture. Repeat: torn up tortillas, beef, sour cream mixture, cheese.

Bake uncovered at 325 degrees for about a half hour, or until the cheese on top is melted and bubbly.

Now here's the fun part. Eat the casserole by scooping it up with tortilla chips!

Delicious, easy, and casual. Enjoy!

Mexican Meatloaf
Matthew Clemons

Ingredients:
- 2 tablespoons olive oil
- 1/2 cup finely chopped onion
- 1 medium carrot, finely diced
- 1 rib celery, finely diced
- 1 garlic clove, minced
- 1 pound lean ground beef
- 6 ounces Mexican chorizo, raw
- 3/4 teaspoons salt
- 1/4 teaspoons ground black pepper
- 1/4 teaspoons cayenne pepper
- 1/2 teaspoons ground cumin
- 2 eggs, beaten
- 1/4 cup ketchup
- 1/4 cup sour cream
- 1/2 cup Panko bread crumbs

Directions:
(The key is the mini-loaf pans.)
Preheat the oven to 375 degrees F.

In a cast iron or heavy skillet, add the oil and heat over medium-high heat. Add the onion, carrot, celery, and garlic. Cook, stirring often, until vegetables are soft, about 6-8 minutes. Set aside until cool.

In a medium bowl, combine the salt, pepper, cayenne pepper, cumin, and eggs. Add the ketchup and sour cream. Mix well with a fork.

In a large bowl, combine the sautéed vegetables, ground beef, and chorizo.

Pour the sour cream mixture on top of the mixed meats. Sprinkle with bread crumbs and mix thoroughly with hands.

Put the mixture into mini loaf pans, filling each about 1/2-2/3 full. Bake until a meat thermometer inserted in the center of the meatloaf registers 160 degrees F., about 30-40 minutes. Remove from the oven and pour off any juices/grease.

Individual meat loaves are ready to slice and serve. They can be cooled in the pans before removal, then frozen.

Skipperlabskovs (Sailor's Stew)
Barbara Allan

Here is an old recipe that Mother brought back from a trip to her native Denmark some years ago. Mother claims to have gotten it from a sailor in Copenhagen, but refused to divulge under what circumstances—which was all right by me because I don't want to know. The fleet was apparently in, which is more than enough information.
—*Brandy*

Ingredients:
- 4 tablespoon. butter
- 1 1/2 pounds boneless beef or veal cut in 1-inch cubes
- 3 onions, chopped
- 3 cups beer or ale
- 3 cups beef bouillon
- 1 teaspoons salt
- 12 peppercorns
- 2 bay leaves
- 6 medium Idaho potatoes, peeled and cut into 1/2-inch cubes
- 2 chopped chives or green onion tops

Preparation:
Melt 4 tablespoon. butter in Dutch oven. Add meat and onions. Cook, stirring frequently, until onions are transparent but not brown. Add beer, bouillon, salt, peppercorns, and bay leaves. Add extra liquid (beer, bouillon or water) if necessary to cover meat. Simmer, covered, over low heat for 20 minutes. Add potatoes and continue covered simmering until meat is tender, about 1 1/2 to 2 hours. Sprinkle each serving with chives. Serves 4 civilians or 2 hungry sailors.

COOKING WITH CRIMESPREE

Submitted by Barbara Allan (Max Allan Collins and Barbara Collins, authors of the Trash 'n' Treasures mystery series, featuring daughter-and-mother sleuthing team, Brandy and Vivian Borne.)

Cod and Bacon-Saffron White Bean Stew
Ro Cuzon

Ingredients:
- 3 thick-cut bacon slices, chopped
- 1 cup sliced shallots
- 3 tablespoons extra-virgin olive oil
- 6 garlic cloves, chopped
- 1 14 1/2 ounce can petite diced tomatoes in juice
- 1 8 ounce bottle clam juice
- 1/3 cup dry white wine
- 1/2 teaspoon saffron threads
- 2 fresh thyme sprigs
- 2 15 ounce cans small white beans, drained
- 1 1/2 pounds cod fillets, cut into 1 1/2-inch chunks
- 1 French baguette

Preparation:
Sauté bacon and shallots in large pot over medium-high heat until bacon is crisp. Add olive oil and garlic; stir 1 minute. Add tomatoes with juice, clam juice, wine, thyme, and saffron; bring to boil. Reduce heat; simmer 5 minutes. Add beans and fish; bring to simmer. Cover; simmer until fish is just opaque in center, about 5 minutes. Season stew to taste with salt and pepper. Serve with plenty of toasted french baguette spears.

NB: you can add some cayenne pepper for heat if you want.

Gluten-Free Stuffed Chicken Breasts
Hilary Davidson

Ingredients:
    Roasted red peppers, in slices
    Boneless skinless chicken breasts (1 per person)
    Dijon mustard
    Fresh basil leaves
    Pine nuts
    Shredded mozzarella
    Black pepper
    Toothpicks

One of the best things about working, years ago, for *Canadian Living* magazine was having the test kitchen on site. I stole this recipe from them, though I've modified it in several ways, because I'm a lazy cook and because I have celiac disease, so I'm on a gluten-free diet. The original recipe told you how to go about roasting the peppers yourself; if you have the time to do that, great! But using pre-roasted peppers from a jar works just as well. Feel free to play with the other ingredients, too. I don't measure things out when I cook—I just use what looks to me like enough. The best thing about this recipe is that it will turn out to be delicious anyway.

Instructions:
1. Using a sharp knife held horizontally, cut chicken almost all the way through; open it like a book (if you accidentally cut it all the way through, don't stress; you'll just need more toothpicks to hold it together while it cooks)
2. Spread mustard on the "inside" part of the chicken breast
3. Put a couple of red pepper pieces inside, then a few basil leaves, then some pine nuts
4. Sprinkle the mozzarella on top of the peppers and basil

5. Now fold the top part of the chicken back on top, and secure it with a couple of toothpicks. Don't worry if some mustard or pine nuts ooze out.

6. Sprinkle each with black pepper. Place under broiler. It takes about 12 minutes to cook. Be sure to turn it over once. When it's done, the chicken should be golden brown outside and no longer pink inside.

Hilary Davidson was a prolific travel journalist before she turned to crime. Her debut novel, The Damage Done *(Forge, 2010), has won an Anthony Award, and the Crimespree debut novel award.*

Spaghetti Sauce and Meatballs
Jim DeFelice

There's nothing very mysterious about this dish, which fed me and a bunch of friends through graduate and is now the go-to dish at home. Make a big batch on Sunday and you'll have sauce for the rest of the week. It's great with any form of dry pasta, though we're partial to spaghetti.

Sauce (Makes a vat of sauce, enough to feed an army, or a half-dozen college kids):

Basic ingredients:
    Olive oil
    1 onion large enough to make your eyes tear when cutting
    1 medium-sized green pepper
    1/2 stalk celery
    As much garlic as you can stand
    2 large cans (28 ounces) of crushed tomatoes
    1 large can (12 ounces) of tomato paste
    1 can of chicken broth
    Water
    A pinch or 2 of Basil (fresh minced herbs are best, but dried are acceptable)
    A pinch or 2 of Oregano
    A sprinkle of Rosemary
    A few snips of Thyme
    Bay leaves
    Salt, pepper
    Meatballs
    A pound of ground chuck, more or less
    Optional ingredients:
    Mushrooms
    Carrot

Wine (dry red, preferably, but whatever you like to drink)
Beef or pork
Grating cheese (Romano or Parmesan)

Preparation:
Start by opening wine and having a good slug. Beer can be substituted, though make sure it doesn't get into the sauce. Stronger liquors are not recommended.

Dice vegetables and garlic and simmer in hot olive oil until tinged brown. I like to use a keg-sized sauce pan for all of this so I don't have too much to clean up.

Add tomatoes, then tomato paste and broth. If adding meatballs or any meat, it's best to thin the sauce by adding a large can's worth of water. If not, add enough water to the tomato paste can to free the good stuff on the bottom, then pour that into the sauce.

Simmer on low heat for as long as you can be patient. (This is why wine helps.) Twenty minutes is the regulation time, but few people have that kind of patience, or that much wine. Continue to stir occasionally, as the heavier parts of the sauce will collect on the bottom and threaten to burn.

Add other liquid ingredients. If adding wine, about a half a cup will do it.

Add herbs to taste. You'll want to experiment with the actual amount; in this size sauce, I'd begin with a soup spoon of basil, slightly little less oregano, and a teaspoon of the others. But then again, I have been known to rip the top off the spice jars and pour away. To my mind, you can never have enough basil.

Stir.

If adding meatballs or other meat, add them now.

Simmer on a very low heat until starving, the longer the better. I stir the pot as often as I can, mostly as a life rule. It's also a good excuse to steal meatballs. Grandma would make the sauce before breakfast and let it "perk" until dinner, checking every so often to make sure the bottom doesn't burn. Caution: If you're not going to check it every so often—if you're going to go work on your novel or cram for an exam—turn the sauce off or it will almost surely burn.

Cheese, if added, should go in about ten minutes before serving. Check seasonings just before serving and adjust if necessary.

Note: The amount of sauce can be easily increased by adding another can (or so) of crushed tomatoes, or, if you're a college student and saving beer money, adding more water. Just keep the proportions roughly the same. The tomato paste thickens the sauce, so if it's too watery for your taste, you can adjust it by adding more.

Croque Monsieur
J.T. Ellison

I've always been a fan of this open-face Parisian classic, and I ate my way through the brasseries and cafes trying as many as I could.

Finding the perfect recipe to share is difficult, for every Croque Monsieur is not created equal. From béchamels and cheeses and breads to the placement of the Dijon mustard, even the number of slices of bread, are rarely agreed upon. Here's one I liked, that's both simple, and tasty, with, of course, some Ellison variations. You'll note this calls for Gruyère cheese, and (gasp) a little Parmesan, or even some grated Grana Padano. I've found this combination gives things a little more flavor, as the traditional Emmental (Swiss) cheese can be somewhat bland.

Ingredients:
2 Tablespoons butter
2 Tablespoons flour
1 cup milk (I prefer unsweetened almond milk)
Salt, freshly ground pepper, and a pinch of nutmeg, to taste
6 ounces Gruyère cheese, grated (about 1 1/2 cups grated)
1/4 cup grated Parmesan cheese (packed)
8 slices of good harvest French or Italian loaf bread
12 ounces baked ham, sliced thin
Good Dijon mustard—I like Maille Dijon

Directions:
Preheat oven to 400 degrees F.
To make the béchamel sauce: Melt butter in a small saucepan on medium/low heat until it just starts to bubble. Add the flour and cook, stirring until smooth, about 2 minutes.

Slowly add the almond milk, whisking continuously, cooking until thick. Remove from heat.

Add the salt, pepper, and nutmeg. Stir in the Parmesan and 1/4 cup of the grated Gruyère. Set aside.

Butter your bread, spread on a baking sheet, and toast them in the oven, a few minutes each side, until lightly toasted.

(Alternatively, you can assemble these as sandwiches, with a top and bottom, and sprinkle the last of the cheese on top before broiling, but everyone I ate was open-face.)

Lightly brush the toasted slices with béchamel and mustard. Add the ham slices and about 1 cup of the remaining Gruyère cheese.

Place on a broiling pan. Bake in the oven for 5 minutes, then turn on the broiler and broil for an additional 3 to 5 minutes, until the cheese topping is bubbly and lightly browned.

If you top this sandwich with a fried egg it becomes a Croque Madame.

Dinner
Christa Faust

Take one sissy slave (preferably one who knows how to cook.)
Add high heels and frilly apron.
Beat until dinner occurs.
Enjoy.

Stride's Chicken
Brian Freeman

A juicy, flavorful chicken dish with lemon and capers that's ready in the time it takes to make pasta.

Serves 2

Ingredients:
- 2-3 boneless skinless chicken breasts
- 1/3 box whole grain rotini pasta
- 1 cup white wine
- Juice of 1 lemon
- Handful of capers
- 1 stick butter, cold, cut into 8 tablespoons
- 2 tablespoons olive oil
- Flour for coating
- Salt and pepper

Preparation:
Start heating water for pasta. Start heating frying pan to medium heat.

While water is heating, gather other ingredients for your mise en place.

Pound chicken breasts to even 1/2-inch height.

Salt and pepper chicken on both sides.

Dredge chicken breasts in flour and shake off excess.

When water is boiling, add olive oil to hot frying pan and add chicken breasts.

Cook chicken breasts on one side, moving occasionally, for about 4 minutes. Should be nice and brown. (After chicken has been cooking for about 3 minutes, add pasta to boiling water)

Reduce heat to low.

Flip chicken breasts and cook about 4 more minutes on other side.

Add white wine and lemon juice to frying pan.

Cover and cook 2-3 more minutes.

Remove cover and remove chicken from pan to separate plate.

Turn off heat on frying pan.

Add capers.

Add butter a couple tablespoons at a time and gently stir to melt.

By the time your butter is incorporated, your pasta should be done. Drain pasta and separate among two bowls. Place 1 or 1 1/2 chicken breasts on top of pasta in each bowl.

Spoon sauce over chicken and pasta.

Reserve any left-over sauce to eat directly from the pan while you are cleaning up.

www.bfreemanbooks.com

Puttanesca Sauce
A variation on a traditional recipe from Siracusa
Jim Fusilli

Ingredients:
   3 cups plum tomatoes seeded and chopped*
   Garlic to taste, sliced thin
   2 tablespoons olive oil
   1/2 cup cured olives, pitted and chopped
   1 teaspoon capers
   1 tablespoon fresh parsley, chopped
   Bay leaf
   Crushed pepper to taste
   1 pound Fusilli Con Buco

Preparation:
Bring water to boil for pasta.
   Heat sauté pan. Reduce heat. Add olive oil. Add garlic, allowing the oil to take on its taste. Don't brown or burn garlic. Add tomatoes carefully. Add bay leaf.
   When tomatoes begin to simmer, add olives. Add capers. Add crushed red peppers. Simmer. (Note: Don't add salt. Cured olives and capers will impart their salt to the sauce.)
   Add pasta to water. When water returns to a boil, add a ladle of its starchy pasta water to tomato-and-olive mixture.
   Drain pasta. Place in serving dish. Ladle sauce over pasta and stir until fusilli is well coated. Sprinkle with fresh parsley.

*If fresh plum tomatoes aren't available in abundance, use canned chopped tomatoes, draining most of the liquid before heating.

Queen Esther's Chicken-N-Dumplins
Daniel J Hale

Serves 4

I began work on this steadfast in the knowledge that the wonderful woman who helped to raise me in the wilds of southern Arkansas had been the originator and perfector of this recipe. One of my sisters told me that it was actually our mother's recipe, and that our mother had always been the one to make the dish. If my sister's right (and she usually is), that's a shame, because incorporating my mom's name into the recipe wouldn't have quite the same poetic ring. So I'm going to pretend my sister never said a word to me about it. Now, without further ado, I give you Queen Esther's Chicken-N-Dumplins.

Ingredients list:
1 pound of boneless, skinless chicken breast
2 cups all-purpose flour
1/2 teaspoon (that's teaspoon, not tablespoon) salt
1/2 cup vegetable shortening (you can substitute butter, all or in part)
A healthy supply of refrigerated water

Here's the chicken part:
Cut the chicken breast into medium-sized pieces and place in a large pot.
Add 3 cups of chilled water.
Bring to a boil and then reduce heat.
Cover and simmer until tender (about 30 minutes).

And here's the dumplings part:

Author's note: I use a stand mixer with a dough hook, but perfect results can also be achieved with a food processor or even via manual labor.

In large mixing bowl, combine 2 cups of flour with 1/2 teaspoon (that's teaspoon, not tablespoon) of salt.

Mixing constantly, cut the shortening and/or butter slowly into the dry ingredients until pea-sized balls bead up.

While still mixing, add 1 tablespoon (not teaspoon) of chilled water at a time until one large dough ball is formed; it should take 6-7 tablespoons of water.

Using a rolling pin and a large, flat, clean surface, roll out the dough until it's pie-crust thin, and then cut it into 1-inch-wide strips.

This is where everything comes together:

Once the chicken is cooked, add one can of Campbell's Cream of Chicken Soup (because this is a recipe from the South).

Add pepper (and maybe a bit of salt) to taste.

Bring the mixture to a boil.

Add dumplings one at a time, stirring constantly (if you throw in all the dumplings at once, you'll end up with a clump of undercooked dough ... and nobody likes that).

Cover and simmer on low for 20-60 minutes (depending on the thickness of the dumplings), stirring occasionally.

Author summation: Back home in Arkansas, chicken-n-dumplins are often served with black-eyed peas and fried okra, but those are recipes for another book. Enjoy!

Almond and Parmesan-Crusted Chicken Thighs
Timothy Hallinan

I use thighs with the bone in for this recipe because they don't dry out like white-meat and boneless cuts do, and I use them with the skin on because that's how I like it, but it works with the skinless, boneless limp shreds of meat that are supposed to keep us alive forever.

You'll need:
- A small handful of uncooked almond slices, or about 4 unroasted almonds
- 1 or 2 cloves of garlic, depending on your tolerance. (You can skip it if you want.)
- 1 1/2 tablespoons of grated Parmesan
- A tablespoon or so of milk (Skim is okay, and so is almond or rice milk as long as it's unsweetened.)
- An egg white
- 1 1/2 tablespoons of mustard, either Dijon or whole-grain mustard (no bright yellow hot-dog mustard)
- 4 chicken thighs, as described above
- Some cooking spray

Preparation:
Heat the oven to 375.

Throw the almond or almond slices and the garlic into a food processor and process them into a coarse, mealy consistency.

On a flat plate, mix the almond-garlic meal and the grated parmesan.

Beat the egg white, the mustard, and milk-of-your-choice in a shallow bowl.

Haul the thighs through the egg mixture to get them sticky and then roll them in the meal to coat both sides. You're after a sort of fried-chicken effect.

Spray an oven-proof skillet, heat it to medium-high, and cook the chicken for about three minutes on a side. (Use a fork to turn it because a spatula will scrape off the coating.)

Put the skillet in the oven and cook it for 12-15 minutes, until the juices produced when a fork is stuck into it are clear.

Remove from the oven and let the chicken rest for five minutes or so.

Eat. Don't talk with your mouth full.

Pulled Pork
Ian Hamilton

Ingredients:
   4-5 pounds pork shoulder, bone-in.
   2 tablespoons of salt
   2 teaspoons of dark sugar
   1 tablespoons of smoked paprika
   2 teaspoons of liquid smoke

Preparation:
Heat oven to 220 degrees C.
Mix salt, sugar and paprika together. Then rub 1/2 of it into the meat.
Put meat into a roasting pan on top of foil, but don't cover.
Cook for 40 minutes.
Take meat from oven and add remainder of salt/sugar/paprika, and add liquid smoke.
Cover meat with aluminum foil.
Reduce oven temperature to 125 degrees C.
Cook meat for 7 hours.
Remove from oven. Remove foil.
Increase oven temperature to 220 again, and cook for 10 minutes.
Remove from oven, cover meat with foil tent, and let rest for 30 minutes.
Then separate with spoon and fork and enjoy.

Bomber Dogs
A recipe from the Stealth Bomber
James Hannibal

Today, the B-2 Spirit—commonly known as the Stealth Bomber—has a microwave oven that enables the pilots to cook meals on long duration missions. These missions routinely extend beyond the 20-hour mark, so the crews naturally get hungry.

However, the microwave is a very recent upgrade. For most of the bomber's 20-year history, stealth pilots had little choice in regards to meals.

Some enterprising aircrews lugged coolers full of sodas and subs on board, usually to discover ten hours later that the ice had melted and the sandwich bags had failed, leaving their subs a little mushy. Those who did not enjoy soggy sandwiches could opt to buy boxed meals—known to pilots as "boxed nasties"— from the flight kitchen. For $5 a pilot could get two pieces of stale bread and a child-sized juice box along with his or her choice of a greenish cold cut, an oldie-moldy chicken breast, or a cheap buffet style cup of generic peanut butter. A bruised apple usually accompanied the mix to appease the flight surgeon—the worm was thrown in for free.

Still, the stealth pilots did have one more, frequently used option: the Bomber Dog.

In place of a microwave, the original Stealth Bomber had a hot water pot—intended by the Cold War era aircraft engineers to give the pilots a source of hot coffee while they were on their way to nuke the Soviets. During my time in the Stealth, we never did nuke the Commies, and we never actually used that pot to make coffee (carrying a thermos is much easier). But— flying tired and totally invisible at highly classified altitudes— we did use the hot pot to make the best chilidogs I've ever eaten.

Ingredients:
- 4 Hot Dogs (2 for each pilot)
- 4 Hot Dog Buns
- 1 15-ounce can of Hormel Chili (2 for 1 at the Base Exchange)
- Toppings to taste

Flight Gear:
- 1 General Electric F118 Engine Generator-Powered Hot Pot (or a 4-quart saucepan)
- 1 Flight Glove with Optional Oil Stains (or paper towels)
- 1 Set of Rusty Pliers From the Cockpit Toolkit (tongs will also work)
- 1 P-38 Keychain Can Opener Banned by the TSA (or a standard kitchen can opener)
- 1 Military Issue Butterfly Handle Stainless Steel Canteen Cup (or a small saucepan)
- 4 Feet of Aluminum Foil

Caveats:

No onions—The B-2 cockpit is incredibly loud due to reflected noise from the buried engines. If the intercom or either headset goes out, pilots have to get nose to nose and shout to be heard. Bad breath kills, Peaches.

No beans in the chili—The B-2 cockpit is poorly ventilated. That's all I'm going to say on that.

Directions:
1. Fill the pot 3/4 full with water and bring to a boil.
2. Add the hot dogs and simmer for 10 minutes
3. While the hot dogs are cooking, lay out four 12-inch sheets of aluminum foil—one sheet for each hot dog bun, and set each bun open at the center of the left edge of its respective sheet. If the buns roll off the foil and onto the floor due to unexpected turbulence, the ten-second rule applies.
4. When the hot dogs are cooked, keep the water simmering. Use the pliers from the toolkit (or tongs if you must) to remove them. Dab the hot dogs on your flight glove (or paper towels) to remove excess water, and then place one hot dog in each bun.

5. Roll each bun from left to right in its aluminum foil. Twist the ends to secure.

6. Place all four wrapped buns in the simmering water. MAKE SURE THE FOIL SEAMS ARE FACING UP (they'll float). Heat for 7 minutes.

7. Use the rusty pliers from the toolkit (or tongs if you're not a glass-eating, grisly bomber pilot) to remove the foil-wrapped buns from the pot, and then remove the pot from the heat. Let the foil wraps cool while you make the chili.

8. HEAT THE CHILI ACCORDING TO THE DIRECTIONS ON THE CAN (using a saucepan or microwave-safe bowl).

However, this is the Stealth Bomber method:

Open the chili with your TSA-banned P-38 keychain can opener and poor it into your standard military issue stainless steel canteen cup. Using the rusty pliers, set the canteen cup in the simmering hot pot to heat for ten minutes or until it melts the plastic spork that came with your boxed nasty. Stir occasionally.

9. Remove the chili from the heat, and then unwrap your hot dogs. Be careful because the inside wrapping will be hot, and there may be steam. The finished bomber dogs will have the look and feel of the hot dogs you get from the roving concessioner at the baseball park. Use the half-melted spork to spoon the chili onto your hot dogs, and add toppings to taste. Remember, no onions.

10. After landing, empty out the hot pot onto the flight line and wipe it clean with your flight glove. This is important, because if the crew chief finds a film of congealed hot dog grease inside the hot pot, you'll owe him a case of Guinness, thus negating the bargain you got on the chili at the Base Exchange.

James R. Hannibal is a former stealth pilot and drone pilot who has been locked up by enemy missiles and has hunted high value targets on two continents. He is the author Shadow Maker *and* Shadow Catcher *from Berkley Books and Brilliance audio.*

Carolyn's Chicken Salad
Carolyn Hart

Ingredients:
- 1 chicken breast with skin
- 1/4 cup green onions chopped
- 1/4 cup green pepper seeded and chopped
- 1/2 cup mayonnaise (I use Hellman's)
- 1/4 cup milk
- 1 teaspoon curry powder

Preparation:
Simmer one boneless chicken breast with skin (seasoned with Seasoning Salt) 25 minutes. Cool, skin, chop. Mix together mayo, milk (use more or less mayo/milk for desired consistency) Mix with chicken, onions, green peppers, and curry. Refrigerate. Serves two.

Stuffed Maine Lobster a la McCabe
James Hayman

When Mike McCabe, the co-hero of my McCabe/Savage thrillers, moved from New York to Maine his definition of great dinner was a blood rare New York Strip steak and a couple of single malt scotches. But after a few years of living in Portland, one of the seafood heavens of the world, he's added a little maritime variety to his life.

One of his new favs is seafood stuffed baked Maine lobster. Here's how to make this very special dish.

Seafood Stuffing For Four Lobsters

Ingredients:
 1 tablespoon butter
 1/4 pound picked-over crabmeat
 6 sea scallops, quartered
 8 raw jumbo shrimp, tailed, deveined and chopped
 1/4 pound cooked lobster meat
 1 1/2 cups crumbled Ritz crackers.
 Lemon juice, for seasoning
 1/4 cup White wine, for seasoning
 Salt and freshly ground black pepper, for seasoning

Method:
Melt butter in saucepan. Add all the seafood to the sauté pan and cook gently for 3 minutes. Mix in wine, lemon juice and crumbled crackers. Season to taste with salt and pepper. Put aside.

Preheat the oven to 450 degrees F.

Place a little water in a pot large enough to hold four 1 1/4 pound lobsters. Bring to a boil, toss in lobsters and steam for five minutes. Remove from pot and rinse in cold water until cool enough to handle.

Cut open each lobster by inserting your knife just below head and cutting down, splitting the belly (body and tail). Remove anything that looks black or green, leaving meat intact. Drain any water.

Push in as much stuffing as will fit. Be generous. Top stuffing with pats of butter

Place the stuffed lobster, stuffing-side-up, in a roasting pan. Add the lemon juice to the bottom of the pan to keep the lobster moist while cooking. Bake for 10 minutes, or just until the claws begin to split. Do not allow the lobster to dry out.

Serve with a good California chardonnay and enjoy.

Kat's Yes-That-Says-Oats Barbecue Meatloaf
Katrina Holm

Ingredients:
   1 pound ground beef
   1 small onion, diced
   1/2 cup quick oats
   1 egg, beaten
   1/2 cup barbecue sauce
   1 teaspoons salt
   1/2 teaspoons pepper

Preparation:
Preheat oven to 375 degrees F. Combine the beef, the onion, the oats, the egg, the salt, the pepper, and 1/4 cup of the barbecue sauce. Shape the mixture into a loaf and place the loaf in a lightly greased baking dish. Evenly coat the loaf with the remaining 1/4 cup barbecue sauce. Bake for about an hour

Chris and Kat's We're-Not-Italian-But-The-Beef-Is Sandwich Recipe
Chris and Katrina Holm

Ingredients:
- 3 pounds beef chuck roast
- 8-10 cloves of garlic
- 1 16-ounce jar sliced pepperoncini peppers
- 1 can beef broth
- 3/4 packet dry Italian dressing mix
- Liquid smoke
- Sub rolls
- Mayonnaise
- Sliced provolone cheese

Preparation:
Peel and smash the garlic cloves. Use a paring knife to cut slits into the roast—as many as you have garlic cloves. Stuff the smashed garlic into the slits you've cut into the roast. Place the roast in your slow cooker. Pour the contents of the jar of pepperoncini peppers over the roast. Add the can of beef broth and approximately 3/4 of the packet of Italian dressing mix. Add several dashes of liquid smoke.

Cover and cook on low for approximately eight hours. Shred the beef with two forks. This is a good time to skim some fat off the liquid in the slow cooker (if you have any interest in doing so). Add the shredded beef back to the liquid in the slow cooker.

Split and toast some sub rolls. Spread mayonnaise on the toasted rolls, and then top the rolls with a mix of shredded beef and pepperoncini peppers. Top whole thing with slices of provolone cheese and place it under the broiler just long enough to melt the cheese. Pour yourself a little bowl of liquid from the slow cooker. Dip your sandwich into the liquid and devour.

Pasta with Sweet "House" Sauce
David Housewright

Recipe:

15 minutes preparation time; 1 hour cooking time. Makes about 6 cups.

Ingredients:
- 2 tablespoons butter
- 2 tablespoons olive oil
- 2 medium carrots chopped
- 1 large yellow bell pepper chopped
- 1 pound sweet ground Italian sausage
- 2 large garlic cloves finely chopped
- 1/2 cup dry red wine
- 2 cans (14.5 ounces each) diced tomatoes (You can substitute 10-12 whole, peeled tomatoes that you dice yourself—if you have the time, it's worth it)
- 1 teaspoon dried oregano
- 1 teaspoon dried sweet basil
- 1-3 tablespoons tomato paste (depending on how thick you like your sauce)

Preparation:
Heat olive oil and butter over medium-high heat in a 2-quart saucepan until butter is melted. Add carrots and bell pepper, stirring frequently until tender-crisp. Add sausage and garlic. Stir frequently until sausage is no longer pink. Add wine. Cook for 3-4 minutes. Add remaining ingredients. Heat to boiling; reduce heat to low, cover and simmer for at least 45 minutes. Serve over pasta of your choice (I recommend penne, mostaccioli, or rotini—something sturdy to stand up to a heavy sauce).

A reformed newspaper reporter and ad man, David Housewright has won an Edgar Award from the Mystery Writers of America as well as three Minnesota Book Awards. His 17th book—Unidentified Woman #15—*will be published in June 2015 (St. Martin's Minotaur).*

Turkey Sandwich
Jon Jordan

With the holidays coming, a staple of the season is the turkey sandwich. I love these for many reasons. It helps get rid of left overs, they are easy to make and eat and they taste so good.

Pretty simple ingredient list.
- Leftover turkey—sliced or in chunks. Deli style will work but not as well.
- White bread—White bread seems to work best, though sour dough and rye are damn good too.
- Mayo—I love the mayo with turkey, sometimes mustard
- Optional—lettuce (crispy), Bacon, cheddar cheese, tomato, bread and butter pickles

Directions
Layout bread, load up with turkey and other ingredients, fold together, eat.

Here's the important part. These sandwiches are best with milk, ice cold. Also the best way to eat them is in a recliner or on a couch, television on with either football or a movie you've seen before. Have a table nearby so you won't have to reach for your food or milk. The reason for the programming choice and positioning when you eat is so that minutes after finishing you can fall asleep into a nice nap, and by having football or a movie you've already watched on you don't miss anything.

When you wake up repeat until all the turkey is gone.

The Perfect Reuben
Jon Jordan

I was taught how to make Reuben's back in my bartending days by a man named Morry Katz who ran a bar in Milwaukee for over thirty years. I liked all the food but the Reuben was always my favorite. It seems simple, but a couple little tricks elevate it to perfect.

Ingredients:
- Corned Beef, preferably sliced at a deli. I usually get a pound to a pound and a half
- Swiss Cheese—1/2 pound
- Rye Bread 8-10 slices
- Sauerkraut 1 can
- Butter

Preparation:
You need two pans. Heat both to a medium heat. Take your sauerkraut and layout in 1 pan, you want it to heat up and cook off a little of the moisture.

Layout out your bread. Put Swiss cheese on both pieces. Quantity depends on taste, I like a little extra because I like the melty effect.

In the second pan heat up the corned beef, not too hot, just enough to take off a little moisture.

Put about three to four tablespoons worth of sauerkraut on 1 slice, put warmed corned beef (I like it about a 1/4 to 1/2-inch thick) on matching slice. Flip together and butter bread, lay buttered side down in med heat pan and butter the side facing up. As cheese starts to melt bread should brown just a bit. Flip over to brown side two, press down just a bit as this will help keep sandwich together.

Serve with either a brown or horseradish mustard or Thousand Island dressing (I like it either way).

I serve with a sharp dill pickle and coleslaw on the side.

It should make between four and five sandwiches.

For a variation try pickled red cabbage instead of sauerkraut and dip in Russian dressing.

Enchiladas De Jo Coque
Jon Jordan

This is a recipe my mother used to cook and it was always a huge hit. The recipe easily multiplies and I recently did it with 12 pounds of chicken. The stock is almost like cooking a chicken soup, though with nothing in it but broth when you are done. I've also on occasion added more cheese or chilies.
It also reheats well.

Ingredients:
    2 pounds of chicken breasts
    2 cups water
    2 large onions,
    1/4 cup coarsely chopped celery leaves,
    4 sprigs fresh parsley
    1 bay leaf, 4-6 peppercorns
    1 teaspoon kosher salt, 3 cups sour cream
    3 tablespoons butter, 4-8 ounces of green chilies
    8 corn tortillas
    12 ounces Monterrey Jack cheese (White Cheddar also works)
    Small can of black olives sliced.

Preparation:
Combine chicken, water in kettle, bring to boil skimming foam as needed. Add celery leaves, parsley, peppercorns salt and bay leaf and reduce heat to simmer. Cook chicken until firm and remove chicken to plate. Strain broth left behind saving juice, reduce to 1 cup.
    Pour stock into bowl and combine with sour cream. Set aside.
    Chop chicken into small pieces (1/2-inch cubes) and brown in light amount of oil for color and texture.

Preheat oven to 375.

Butter sides and bottom of 9x13-inch pan (Pam works also).

Melt 2 tablespoons of butter in pan, add chopped onions, cook till soft. Stir in chilies transfer to bowl. Add chicken and sour cream mix and fold together.

Heat tortillas in a dry pan till soft.

Take 1/3 cup chicken mixture and wrap in tortilla. Place in two rows in bottom of buttered pan. Pour remaining sour cream mix over top. Shred cheese and sprinkle over top and add olives to top.

Bake for 20 minutes and serve with refried beans.

Judy Bobalik's Upside-Down Pizza
As cooked by Ruth Jordan

Ingredients
  2 teaspoons olive oil
  1 pound any meat, casing removed (if sausage)
  1 cup onion, sliced
  8 ounces mushrooms, sliced
  1 cup pasta sauce
  1 cup pizza sauce
  1/2 cup black olives, sliced
  16 ounces mozzarella cheese, shredded
  2 eggs
  1 cup milk
  1 tablespoon olive oil
  1 cup all-purpose flour
  1/2 teaspoon salt
  1/4 cup Parmesan, grated

Directions
Preheat oven to 400 degrees F.
  Heat oil in large skillet over medium heat. Add meat and cook for 3 minutes or until browned and cooked through, breaking up the meat as it cooks with a wooden spoon. Add onion and mushrooms and cook 2 minutes, until soft. Add pasta sauce, pizza sauce and olives and bring to a simmer, about 2 minutes. Remove from heat and transfer sauce to the bottom of a 9x13-inch baking dish. Top with mozzarella cheese.
  In a medium bowl, whisk together eggs, milk and oil until blended. Whisk in flour and salt until well blended. Pour mixture over sauce in pan. Sprinkle with Parmesan. Bake 25 minutes, or until golden brown. Let stand for 5 minutes before slicing and serving.

COOKING WITH CRIMESPREE

As with every tried and true recipe, this one has a story. I was looking for a quick dinner and Judy pointed out I could use any meat, substitute a sauce, take out mushrooms and add another veggie. This is a recipe to play with your leftovers and it's always delicious. So delicious, that when company is coming I suggest making two. So yes, Judy has saved my ass in the kitchen, too.

Shakshouka
A North African egg dish
Andrew Kaplan

Serves 2—4, depending upon portion size.

Ingredients:
- 1/2 dozen large eggs
- 2 regular size fresh tomatoes
- 1/2 green pepper
- 1/2 cup of fresh sliced mushrooms
- 1/2 raw onion
- 1 large slice of Swiss cheese—approximately 1 ounce (or cheese of your choice, but should not be too pungent or strong to overwhelm the other flavors; Swiss is perfect)
- 1 tablespoon olive oil (sufficient to coat a large frying pan)

To prepare:
1. Dice the onion and sprinkle it into a frying pan.
2. Dice the tomatoes, green peppers and mushrooms. Keep each separate.
3. Cut up the Swiss cheese into roughly 1/2-inch squares.
4. Break and wisk the eggs in a bowl.
5. Add water into the frying pan and heat (so it is at least 1/2-inch deep). This steams the onions, but be sure to turn the heat off before the onions start to brown or burn. Drain any excess water from the frying pan, but leave the onions in the pan.
6. Add the olive oil to the frying pan and use it to coat the frying surface on the bottom and sides.
7. Add the diced green peppers, tomatoes and mushrooms. Mix and heat on a moderate heat.

8. Just as the onions or green peppers start to brown, pour the mixed eggs into the frying pan.

9. Sprinkle the Swiss cheese over the mix.

10. Remove from heat when the eggs are ready to serve.

11. Drain any excess olive oil or liquid.

12. Salt and pepper to taste and serve with the bread of your choice.

Les's Summer Pasta
Leslie Klinger

Known at the local deli (where I cook sometimes) as "Les's Summer Pasta," this is a casual dish, best when the weather is warm and perhaps paired with a meat dish, although it's filling in itself. This will serve a hungry pair of folks or probably 4 people as a side dish.

Ingredients (sorry for the inexactitude of quantities—that's how I cook!):
- A dozen or so firm (but not hard) Italian (plum) tomatoes
- Head of garlic (hey, I use chopped from a jar)
- Basil (fresh)
- Mozzarella (shredded is ok)
- High-quality extra-virgin olive oil (this is for eating, not cooking, so we want it to taste good)
- 1/2 pound Cappellini (angel's hair pasta, preferably fresh if you know how to make your own)

Preparation:
1. Prep the tomatoes—we're going to "concassé" them. This is chef talk for "peel and pulp the tomatoes." The technique is as follows:

    a. First, slice off the stem-top of the tomato, then make a small "x" with a sharp knife on the pointed bottom.

    b. Boil enough water to immerse the tomatoes.

    c. Immerse the tomatoes for a few minutes, until the skin is loosened (the tips of the "x" will peel back). Don't let the tomatoes cook.

    d. Remove the tomatoes quickly with a slotted spoon and immerse them in ice water, to prevent cooking. Remove skin. If done properly, it should slide right off, but you may need to use a sharp knife to help peel off the skin.

e. Halve the tomatoes vertically and, holding each half under running cold water, use your fingers to remove the seeds and pulp (but not the "meat"—the internal ribs)

2. Once the tomatoes have had their skin, seeds, and pulp removed, chop them into small, finger-tip size pieces. Set aside in a bowl

3. Chop the basil leaves. I prefer julienning (roll the leaves and then slice them into tiny "strings" of basil).

4. Chop (or slice thinly, if you're into Goodfellas) however much garlic you prefer. I use a half dozen cloves or probably a tablespoon of pre-chopped, but I love garlic! No garlic-press, please.

5. Toss the tomatoes with chopped basil leaves, chopped garlic, a handful of shredded mozzarella, and olive oil (quantities to taste)

6. Let the mix sit for a while at room temperature, for the flavors to meld

7. Prepare the cappellini. When you remove the pasta from the water, immediately add a little olive oil to prevent it from sticking. Put the pasta in a large pasta bowl (to mix and serve).

8. When the cappellini is cooked, immediately toss it with the tomato mix. The mixture should be distributed nicely throughout the pasta. The heat of the cappellini will cause the cheese to melt. We're not going for lumps here though, so try to toss the mix thoroughly.

9. Serve immediately. The result will be room temperature pasta, flavorful and light!

Searing Salmon
Julie Kramer

A meal time thriller: "She thought it was just dinner with a nice guy; little did she know there was something fishy about him."

2 pounds wild caught Alaskan salmon fillets, cut to suit

Mix together for Marinade:
   1/4 cup brown sugar
   1/4 teaspoons Paprika
   2 garlic cloves, pressed
   2 tablespoons olive oil
   Ground pepper to taste
   Sea salt to taste
   1 tablespoon soy sauce
   1 tablespoon water
   Squeeze lemon wedge

Preparation:
Spread marinate over salmon, cover and refrigerate for a couple hours.
Sear salmon on very hot grill, skin side up, for eye-catching grill marks. Cook about five minutes, then turn fillet, cooking another five minutes or so, depending on thickness until fish is firm.

Author of Stalking Susan, Missing Mark, Silencing Sam, Killing Kate, Shunning Sarah *and* Delivering Death.

Shrimp Jambalaya
William Kent Krueger

So, okay, maybe my favorite recipe. Easy, and when I serve it, folks are fooled into thinking I actually know what I'm doing in a kitchen.

Makes 6 Servings

Ingredients:
    2 pounds raw shrimp, unpeeled
    1/4 cup butter or margarine
    2 medium onions, chopped
    1 green bell pepper, chopped
    2 tomatoes, seeded and chopped
    1 rib celery, chopped
    2 teaspoons salt
    Freshly ground black pepper, to taste
    1/2 teaspoon dried thyme
    Hot pepper sauce, to taste
    1 cup uncooked rice
    1 cups chicken broth

Preparation:
Shell and devein shrimp, set aside. Melt butter in a large saucepan. Add onions, bell pepper, tomatoes and celery, cook 10 minutes, or until vegetables are soft but not browned. Add reserved shrimp, salt, pepper, thyme, and a dash of hot pepper sauce. Cook over medium heat about 5 minutes, or until shrimp turn pink. Add rice and chicken broth. Bring to a boil, stirring once; reduce heat to medium-low. Simmer, covered, 20 minutes, or until rice is cooked. Serve immediately.

Baked Chicken Breasts
Sharon Lynch

Ingredients:
    6 boneless half chicken breasts
    2 cups sour cream
    1/4 cups lemon juice
    4 teaspoons Worcestershire sauce
    4 teaspoons celery salt
    2 teaspoons paprika
    1/2 teaspoons pepper
    4 garlic cloves garlic, finely chopped
    1 3/4 cup bread crumbs
    1/2 cup butter/shortening

Preparation:
1. In large bowl, combine sour cream, lemon juice, Worcestershire sauce, celery salt, paprika, garlic, pepper
2. Add chicken to mixture, coating each piece.
3. Refrigerate, covered, over night.
4. Next day, preheat oven to 350 degrees.
5. Remove coated chicken; Roll each piece in bread crumbs.
6. Melt butter/shortening in baking pan and place chicken.
7. Bake about 1 hour or until chicken is tender.

Stovies
Stuart MacBride

This has to be one of the most iconic dishes in Scotland, and a hell of a lot nicer than our official national dish—deep-fried pizza. Stovies: a thick gloopy unctuous meaty blend of leftover roast lamb, onions and tatties. You can tell it oozes Scottishness, because it's got tatties in it. Not 'potatoes', tatties. Get that bit right and you're halfway there.

Now, true stovie experts are able to time it perfectly, so that the tatties at the bottom catch and impart a smokiness to the dish, but don't worry about that. Even without caught tatties, this is a big steaming pile of hug on a plate.

What goes in them can lead to fist-fights and families never speaking to each other again. Feuds that last generations have been sparked by a suspect plate of this iconic dish. Some people will tell you that stovies should be made with beef, or corned beef, or pork, or leftover curry, but they're liars and deviants and should be shunned. Lamb is the only acceptable meat here. Accept no substitutes.

Then there's the heated topic of how you should eat them. I'm a beetroot man. My wife's all about the oatcakes. And her mother—who is clearly very wrong in the head—thinks it's socially acceptable to dip spoonfuls of stovies into a glass of milk before eating them. Then she drinks the sludgy meaty tattie-clogged milk. Apparently it's a Fife thing. *shudder*

Anyway, leaving such horrors behind us, first we need leftover roast lamb:
SLOW ROAST LEG OF LAMB
1 whole leg of lamb, bone in
3 or 4 large onions, thinly sliced
1 large glass of vermouth

Butter
Salt and pepper

How big your leg of lamb is will depend on the time of year, but that's okay. This isn't crystal meth we're making here. You can approximate a lot of this without causing an explosion or getting arrested.

Preheat your oven to 120 degrees Celsius (250 degrees F).

Get yourself a deep roasting dish that will fit the leg of lamb reasonably snugly and drizzle a little oil in the bottom. Rapeseed's good for this.

Now scatter the finely sliced onions across the bottom of the dish.

Wash and pat dry your leg of lamb and place it on the bed of onions.

Smear the lamb with salted butter and season with salt and pepper.

Add a generous glass of vermouth to the dish.

Now all you've got to do is cover it tightly in tinfoil and stick the whole thing in the oven for six or seven hours. If your oven's a traitorous lump of evil metal like mine, it's not a bad idea to check how it's going after five hours.

By the time it's finished cooking it'll be unctuous and moist, and you should be able to carve it with a spoon. There's going to be a goodly amount of tasty juices in the pan, but probably quite a bit of fat too—this is a good thing! Skim the fat from the juices and when it's cool pop it in the fridge. We'll need it later.

Serve your tasty slow roast lamb with mash and whatever else you like.

Okay, so now we've got lovely leftover lamb. It's much easier to pick the bone clean while the lamb is still warm-ish. As it cools the fat and connective tissue in the meat will firm up and it's more of a pain to get those tasty nuggets of dead baby sheep off. You're looking for bite-sized chunks. Pop the picked meat in a container, top it with any leftover onions from the bottom of the dish, and pour in any of the meat juices you've not scarfed. Keep the bone too. Refrigerate.

Stovies
  Leftover slow-roast leg of lamb (picked)
  3 or 4 white onions, chopped
  The lamb leg bone
  A bag of floury tatties—Maris Piper or King Edwards are good
  Lamb stock
  Pickled sliced beetroot and oatcakes to serve

Get yourself a nice large pot—about big enough to fit a baby—and prepare your tatties. Some people peel theirs, but I wash mine, then score the skins with one of those julienne peelers. Yeah, it's a bit of a faff, but it means you get a much more whoomphy tattie taste in the finished dish. The amount of tatties you need depends on the size of your pot. Use your best judgement, I trust you.

Cut your tatties into chunks.

Pop a good couple of tablespoons of the reserved lamb fat into the pot and melt it over a medium to high heat, then add the onions. Fry them till they're lovely and golden, and beginning to caramelise. Now tip in your tatties and stir to coat them with all that lovely lamb fat and onion. Season with salt and pepper.

Add the bone to the pot. I like to sever it at the knuckle, because it fits better.

Then cover the tatties with lamb stock, and chuck in any leftover onions from the slow roast—I know this sounds like a lot of onions, but they've already had seven hours in a low oven and they're going to melt into a wonderfully savoury smush.

Now it's just a case of leaving the pot to simmer away till the tatties are done. They should be falling apart around the edges. It'll take about twenty to twenty five minutes, but the tatties will know when they're done.

Take the bone out and if you fancy a little extra richness, scoop out the marrow and add it back to the pot.

Stir the tatties, breaking some of them up, then chuck in the lamb to heat through.

Don't worry if your stovies look a bit like soup at this point—you can always spoon out the extra liquor to get a texture you're happy with (not surprisingly, the removed liquid tastes great). The more you stir it, the more mashed the tatties will be. Me? I like it to be firm enough not to ooze across the plate, with the occasional chunk of bite-sized tattie still just holding onto its form.

Have a last taste for seasoning, then serve in a lovely dollopy mound with the pickled beetroot and oatcakes. It goes very well with a nice dram of whisky too. Mmmm...

Lamb Hash

I have no idea why it took me so long to try this, but leftover stovies are tremendous for breakfast if you chuck them in a non-stick pan and fry them till they've got a lovely crispy golden skin. Serve with poached eggs and hot sauce. And maybe some more beetroot.

Right after we sent this off to press Stuart contacted us with this news: "The stovie recipe I sent you has just won me the World Stovie Championship."

Tater Tot Casserole
Kate Malmon

Growing up in the Midwest, I've consumed my fair share of one-dish meals held together by cream of mushroom soup. (God bless the creator of cream of mushroom soup!) To me, there is no greater comfort food than a good casserole. Meat + some kind of starch + cream of mushroom soup = home.

At home in Wisconsin, these meals were always called casseroles. When I moved to Minnesota, these comforting, stick-to-your-ribs meals were suddenly called "hot dish". The difference between the two was never really clear, so I continue to make casseroles and refuse to call my meals "hot dishes".

The following is the casserole recipe my mom baked to win my dad's heart, and the same one I used to snag Dan. Maybe you can use it to win the affections of that someone special and then, since this recipe is for a mystery magazine, kill them and collect the insurance money.

Ingredients:
    1 pound ground beef
    1 small onion, chopped
    1 can of corn, drained
    1 can of sliced mushrooms, drained
    1 can of cream of mushroom soup
    3/4 cup of milk
    1 bag of tater tots

Preparation:
Preheat oven at 350 degrees. Brown ground beef and onion until the beef is no longer pink; drain. In a bowl, combine the corn, mushrooms, and cream of mushroom soup. Rinse out the soup can with the milk and add to the bowl. Add the ground beef and onion to the soup mixture.

Line the bottom of a lightly greased 9x13-inch pan with half of the tater tots. Cover with the meat and soup mixture and add the remaining tater tots to the top. Bake for 1 hour.

Maw McLean's "Posh" Stovies
Russell McLean

It came as a surprise to me when I had to explain to Jen Jordan (your Crimespree special features editor and professional madwoman) what stovies were. I'd been back home to my parent's house, and we'd converted a venison stew into what I referred to as "Posh stovies"—whence came the reply to, "what the heck are stovies?"

It's a tough thing to explain to anyone when you've accepted them as a part of life—from the stodgy end-of-delivery-route disasters that were primary school dinners to the sheer delight of proper, home-made stovies that reaffirmed your faith in Scots cooking (but that's no surprise, cos it was you mum who made them)—but essentially, stovies are leftovers. Traditionally served on a Monday in many Scottish households, where the "leftover cooked meat" was re-used one last time.

So next time you have some kind of leftover stew (impossible, I know, if you happen to be eating with Jon Jordan—chances are he'll find a space for the leftovers before you even have a chance to say, stovies), why not give Maw McLean's version of stovies a quick try.

With many thanks to my mum for actually passing on the recipe:

 Ingredients (serves 4):
 450g potatoes
 1 large onion
 Oil (dripping is traditionally used, but how many of us have beef dripping just lying around the house these days?)
 Salt and Pepper
 1/4 pint good rich gravy
 Leftover cooked meat (venison is good)

Preparation:
Peel the potatoes and slice thickly. Peel the onion and slice thinly. Heat the oil in a heavy pan, add the onion and fry for a few moments to soften. Add the sliced potatoes and turn them in the hot oil. Season with salt and pepper and add the meat and gravy. There should be just enough to cover the base of the pan to prevent the stovies from sticking.

Cover with a tight fitting lid and cook very gently for 30 to 40 minutes. Shake the pan occasionally to stop any sticking but try to keep the lid on. The potatoes should be soft and starting to break up. Serve very hot.

In the aforementioned "posh" stovies, leftover venison stew was used, which made the whole damn thing especially delicious, but you can use whatever meat you like. Beef I think is traditional. I suppose there are probably vegetarian options, too, but... seriously... I am a dedicated carnivore.

You'll probably want to serve it up with some vegetables including chopped and boiled carrots and cabbage. This vegetable aspect is probably quite important as many recent reports have claimed that Scots cooking is incredibly unhealthy. But then those reports are usually made by English busybodies, so what do they know?

Enjoy.

Duck A'L'Orange with Honey Glazed Carrots and Potatoes
Russel D McLean

I know, I know... sounds fancy, doesn't it? Complicated, too. But trust me when I tell you that cooking is not about being fancy, it's about being tasty. And outdated and/or posh as this may sound, it's simple, easy and absolutely delicious. This is one of the simplest things that you can do with duck breast, adding some unexpected flavour with the orange. Duck is one of the best meats you can eat, seconded only by a fine, fine (and well cooked) cut of steak or maybe a deliciously cooked hunk of lamb. Believe me when I say, I'm drooling just thinking about it. I can't resist picking up duck when I see it, whether it's a nice, juicy leg or a delicious breast, the meat has a unique and tantalising flavour that works with a large variety of dishes. And, despite what you may think, it can be very easy to cook. In total this dish takes about 45 minutes to an hour including preparation. And a good chunk of that is waiting for the carrots and potatoes during which time you can sample the wine.

We have a gas cooker. With an electric cooker, I'd imagine you're talking somewhere around 230 rather than gas 7. You may have to experiment a bit. That's how I tend to work with cooking.

For 2 (Generally I cook for myself and the literary critic; for more people, you'll need more ingredients...)

Hint 1: prepare the potatoes and carrots first as they take longer to cook. I tend to use the same tray for both of them, just because my oven's very small. I think the flavours tend to mix nice when you do that.

Hint 2: When I say let the meat rest for five minutes, I mean it. It's something so many people forget when it comes to meats like steaks, lamb and duck. Letting the meat rest really intensifies those flavours.

For the carrots:
   Some carrots
   Honey
   Olive oil
   Salt and Pepper

Slice your carrots into batons. Put them in a bowl, salt and pepper them and mix them with the honey. Stick them on a baking tray and shove in the pre-heated oven for 35-45 minutes around gasmark 7 or 8.

For the potatoes:
   Potatoes
   Garlic
   Olive Oil
   Salt and Pepper

Slice your potatoes into chips (generally speaking you should quarter them). Slice and dice one or two cloves of garlic. Stick them on a baking tray (I'd use the same one for the potatoes and the carrots). Salt and pepper. Glug some olive oil over the top. Shove them in that oven again for 35-45 minutes.

For the duck A'L'Orange
   2 Duck breasts
   1 large orange
   Red wine
   Chicken stock
   Salt
   Pepper
   Olive oil

Squeeze out all the juice from your orange into a jug ready for use. Slice a good quantity of zest from the skin and drop it into the juice. Leave this for now.
Take your duck breasts, salt and pepper them. Heat up some olive oil in a pan on a fairly high heat until it's nice and hot and drop in the ducks, fat side down. Let them cook for about 4 or 5 minutes, turn them over and cook again for another 2 to 3

minutes. Remove them from the pan to an oven proof dish and pop them in a pre-heated oven, somewhere around gas mark 7 or 8 for 8-10 minutes.

Take out the duck and put it to rest for five minutes. This is important. Letting meat rest allows the flavours to spread through the meat. Then, slice the duck breasts into equal slices (they should be golden outside and a gentle pink inside—it is perfectly safe and delicious to eat rare duck but you can cook it for longer to get the meat medium or well done) and get them on your plate with the by-now ready carrots and potatoes.

During that five minutes resting you should reheat that pan which should now have the oil and the juices from the duck swilling around nicely. Put in the orange juices with the zest, and let it start bubbling away. Then the chicken stock. And finally a massive splash of that wine. Let it all bubble away and froth up and turn into a delicious sauce. Pour it over the duck.

Serve.

Eat.

And drink the remainder of that red wine.

Russel D Mclean is the author of five Crime Novels featuring Scottish Private Eye J McNee as well as a variety of short stories. He regularly reviews crime fiction for the Scottish Herald. In past lives, he's been a bookseller, a burger flipper, a webzine editor and a philosophy undergraduate. He lives in Glasgow. www.russeldmcleanbooks.com. @russeldmclean.

Pork Pie á la Val
Catriona McPherson

Back in the old country, making my own pork pie would seem as odd as making my own cornflakes, but here in the West I have learned new skills, like many a pioneer woman before me.

I'm not going to lie to you: this isn't a quick chuck-it-together, but more of a recipe for a wet weekend in a warm kitchen with a talking book. It's not difficult or fiddly though and the results will amaze. I made it for Val McDermid, she shared it with some neighbours and apparently there are now several men in a village in Northumberland who're willing to marry me, no photo necessary. This pie is that good.

Serves 12

Ingredients:
For the pastry:
   1/2 a cup of lard, in cubes
   1/2 a cup of butter, in cubes
   A very scant cup (actually .85) of water
   A scant 2 1/2 cups of flour
   1 1/2 teaspoons salt
   2 beaten eggs
   1 egg to seal and glaze

For the filling:
   2 pounds of pork shoulder, cut into very small cubes
   1/2 pound pork belly, minced
   1/2 pound salt pork, pancetta or bacon, finely chopped
   12 sage leaves, finely chopped
   The leaves from a large sprig of thyme, finely chopped
   1 teaspoon of salt
   2 teaspoons of coarsely ground black pepper

COOKING WITH CRIMESPREE

1/2 teaspoon of mace
A pinch of cayenne pepper
1 bay leaf

For the jelly:
2 pigs' feet,
4 pounds of pork bones
1 large onion, halved but unpeeled
1 carrot, scrubbed and split lengthways
1 stick of celery, split lengthways
A good handful of parsley including the stalks
2 or 3 garlic cloves unpeeled
A scattering of whole black peppercorns

You will also need an 8-inch spring form tin.

Day 1.
Make the stock for the jelly. Pack all the jelly ingredients neatly in a large pot and cover with water. Bring to the boil, reduce the heat and simmer for four to five hours. This could be done in a crock pot. Then strain the stock, discard the bones and vegetables, season with salt, cool the liquid and refrigerate it overnight. The next day, all the fat will have risen to the surface and can be lifted off and thrown away.

Day 2.
Make the pastry.
Put the lard, butter and water in a pan and heat gently without boiling until the fats are melted. Put the flour and salt in a mixing bowl, make a dip in the middle and add the beaten eggs. Stir them around gently with a knife until they are half-mixed but still lumpy. Pour in the melted fat and water and mix together with your fingers to form a dough. It will be very soft. Knead it gently, adding more water if it seems stiff and more flour if it is too sticky to handle. When it's all thoroughly mixed and smooth, wrap it in clingfilm and chill it in the fridge for at least an hour.
Build the pie.

Keep a quarter of the dough in the fridge and roll out the rest on a floured surface until it is 1/4-inch thick and big enough to line the tin. Wrap it around the rolling pin and unfurl it in the tin, pressing it well into the sides. Thoroughly combine all the filling ingredients except the bay leaf and put inside the pastry. Push the bay leaf into the middle. Try to leave a dent in the middle of the mixture, rather than a peak, to help with the addition of the jelly later.

Roll out the remaining quarter of the pastry to make a lid. Brush the edges of the pie base with beaten egg, cover with the lid and crimp together to seal. Cut a round 1/4-inch hole in the top.

Cook the pie.

Place the tin in the middle of a moderate oven (350F) and bake for 30 minutes. Then turn the oven down to 320F and continue to bake for another hour and a quarter. Take pie out, stand the tin on an upturned cup and release the spring. The sides of the tin should drop away. If not, gently ease the pie free with a palette knife. Now brush the top and sides with the rest of the egg glaze and return it to the oven for 15 minutes.

Jelly!

When the pie is cooler but not cold, warm 1/2 a pint of the jellied stock and pour it into the hole in the middle of the pie, using a funnel or a turkey baster. You might have to ease the pastry upwards with the tip of a knife. Tilt the pie this way and that to help the stock disperse and keep trying to get in a little more and a little more until it starts to overflow.

Finally, cool the finished pie and refrigerate it. It will keep—opened or unopened—for 2 weeks. Pork pies are traditionally eaten cold with relish, pickled onions and salad. Enjoy.

Six Hour Pork
Catriona McPherson

At least five and a half of the six hours are hands-free, making this the perfect main dish for a large gathering. You can get swanky with the rest of the meal—spinning sugar baskets and moulding terrines—knowing that, meanwhile, this flavour fiesta is taking care of itself and can't go wrong.

Ingredients:
- A large shoulder of pork. Big as they go. Rolled and tied is ideal but scruffy works too.
- 2 large green apples
- A large glass of sweet sherry, hard cider, sweet wine, marsala—booze, basically.
- 3 cloves of garlic
- A bunch of sage leaves
- A glug of olive oil
- Salt and pepper

Advance:
You will need a deep ovenproof dish, with a close-fitting lid or some additional tough tinfoil, or a crockpot.

Take the pork out of the fridge an hour before you start cooking to let it come up to room temperature.

Set the oven to 300F/150C.

Method:
Peel and grate/pound/press the garlic. Snip the sage leaves up small, then mix together with salt, pepper and oil to make a paste.

Peel, core and slice the apples and lay them in the bottom of the dish.

Lay the pork on top, skin side up. Rub the seasoned oil paste all over the pork, poking it into any gaps. You can slit the surface and push some down into the meat if you like.

Pour the booze and half as much water again into the dish, then cover it tightly. If the lid of your dish isn't great, make an extra seal with foil. Do not wrap the meat closely, though.

Whack it in the oven and leave it for six hours. If you're using a crock-pot, set it on low and no harm will come to it for ten.

After cooking, lift the meat out onto a plate and let it rest in a warm place, covered with foil.

Strain everything else through a sieve, mashing the apple pulp well. (This is the fancy version; it gets rid of bits of skin and sage stalks. I usually don't bother).

It's not a bad idea to get some of the fat off the top of the resulting apple gravy. Use a fat-separating jug if you have one, or put the gravy in the freezer to chill quickly then lift the fat off the top, or lay sheets of kitchen paper on the surface to soak some of it away. Taste it to adjust the seasoning. It might need more salt, some sugar, a squirt of lemon. It might even need some water if it's too rich.

You can "carve" the meat with a spoon. It's delicious served with couscous, rice, noodles, chunky bread (anything bland that soaks up gravy) and plain steamed green vegetables.

Variation: six hour lamb—use a shoulder of lamb, dried peaches instead of apples (and double the amount of water), red wine or port as the booze and rosemary in place of the sage. Serve with couscous or rice.

Another variation: six hour beef—use a fatty brisket or a shin, onions and chunks of root vegetable (sweet potato, parsnip, rutebaga) instead of apples, Guinness as the booze, and a mixture of parsley, oregano and nutmeg in place of the sage. Serve with potatoes.

First Date Beef with Wine & Noodles
Randy Susan Myers

I am not positive that my husband asked me to marry him because it's the first dish I ever cooked for him, but I think it's a distinct possibility. And I must feel a deep sentimental regard for this dish, because at a recent dinner with my daughter Becca and her friends Sophie and Dave, I found myself defending the dish against Sophie's beef stew—and I've never even tasted hers. Sorry, Sophie.

Where I came up with this dish, I have no idea. It's not that special vis-à-vis ingredients, but somehow it all equals smooth, delicious, and singular in flavor. I used it in The Comfort of Lies. When Juliette is depressed, she turns to this dish:

Supper should have tasted like ashes that night, but instead compliments flew as Nathan and her sons forked up buttered noodles, beef chunks, and carrots so tender from wine and time, you'd think they'd been cooked with love.

Thankfully, each time I've cooked this for Jeff, it has been cooked with love. Now, let's see how well I can translate the recipe from my head, heart, and hands to the computer keys. This recipe is for those comfortable in playing with amounts!

Ingredients:
- 1 large onion
- 1 small bag of sweet carrots (or as many as you like)
- 1 box mushrooms sliced (if you like mushrooms)
- 1-2 pounds best quality stew beef or sirloin tips
- 1 bottle good red wine or sherry (depending on your taste)
- 1 carton chicken stock
- Butter or olive oil (butter is richer)
- Egg noodles

A bit of flour
A bit of milk or cream

Preparation:
Sauté onions, carrots and mushrooms for about five minutes, until a bit tender. Dredge beef pieces in flour and add to sautéed mix—stir as you sauté the beef, to prevent it from sticking.

Add a mix of chicken stock and wine to cover—amount of each depending on your taste (I like it very winey). Simmer (add spice if you like—I only use a dash of salt) until beef and carrots are very tender (a few hours or so). When the flavors are married and the beef is soft, make a roux with flour, liquid and a bit of milk or cream and slowly stir into the pot. Thicken to your taste.

Serve over hot buttered egg noodles.

Incredibly Good Mystery Pasta Soup
Vegetarian or Not—Your Choice
Randy Susan Myers

The mystery is how I invented this soup. I suspect it came from a confluence of events: A need to give my husband pasta—it soothes him. A need for something vaguely healthy. My desire for soup. And a lack of a well-stocked larder. The soup that was borne—accidental genius.

Ingredients:
- 1 large onion
- Small bag of baby carrots
- Mushrooms (if you like them)
- Sweet Italian turkey sausage (if desired)
- 2-3 boxes of good chicken or vegetable stock
- 1 jar good tomato sauce
- 1-2 cans of black beans
- Salt to taste
- A bit of wine if you like

Preparation:
Sauté first three ingredients in olive oil for five minutes. (If adding sausage, slice into small discs and sauté with vegetables)

Add stock, tomato sauce, black beans, salt and wine (if desired)

Cook until it seems melded together.

Add: the noodles from 1 box of Annie's Whole Wheat Pasta

As the noodles cook (5 minutes or so) take the package of cheese powder from package and mix with soup liquid to make roux. Pour back into soup.

I add Parmesan cheese (freshly grated) to soup and sprinkle more on top when served.

Dorothy Weathers' Famous Chili Mac
Jenny Milchman

Ingredients:
  1 package ground beef
  1 onion, diced
  1 teaspoon oil
  1 block orange cheddar, grated
  3 tablespoons butter or margarine
  2 tablespoons flour
  1 cup milk
  1 box noodles of your choice
  1 tablespoon tomato paste

Preparation:
Step 1: Cook onion in oil until soft
Step 2: Add ground beef and brown
Step 3: In separate pan, melt butter, stir together with flour
Step 4: Add milk, cook, stirring, until thickened
Step 5: Sprinkle cheese over milk mixture and melt
Step 6: Cook pasta and mix with cheese sauce, ground beef, tomato paste
Step 7: Combine all ingredients and bake at 350 degrees till crispy on top

Dorothy sometimes crumbles Ritz crackers on top of the casserole before she bakes it.

Dorothy Weathers is the wife of the police chief, one of the central, but shadowy, characters in my debut novel, Cover of Snow (Ballantine, 2013). At the end of the novel, my heroine is in a hospital bed, and Dorothy brings her this casserole. The reason she does so has roots in an incident that took place over twenty-five years ago.

Jenny Milchman is the author of the Mary Higgins Clark award-winning novel, Cover of Snow, *and the Indie Next Pick follow-up,* Ruin Falls. *Jenny is the founder of Take Your Child to a Bookstore Day, and Vice President of Author Programs for International Thriller Writers. When she isn't writing, she's out on the road on what Shelf Awareness calls "the world's longest book tours".*

Killer Sloppy Joes
Debi Murray

Mix this all together in a dutch oven.
   20 ounces bottle of catsup
   1 cup of Vidalia onion BBQ sauce (I used Sweet Baby Rays)
   Quarter cup packed brown sugar
   1 teaspoons minced garlic
   Half teaspoon salt
   Quarter teaspoon ground pepper

Chop fine and fry in 2 tablespoons of oil until soft:
   Medium sized onion
   2 stalks celery
   Small red pepper

Add to Dutch oven and mix well.
3 pounds very lean ground beef, fry and drain, then add to Dutch oven.
Mix well and simmer for twenty minutes.
Best damn sloppy joe you will ever taste!

Becca Dapkin's Chicken Tetrazzini
Kill 'Em With Cayenne
Gail Oust

Ingredients:
- 1 (7 ounces) package linguine
- 1 (8 ounces) package of fresh mushrooms, sliced
- 2 tablespoons butter
- 3 cup cooked chicken, chopped
- 1 (10 3/4 ounces) can cream of mushroom soup
- 1 jar of Alfredo sauce (can substitute a container of refrigerated)
- 1/2 cup chicken broth
- 1/4 cup Marsala wine
- 1/4 teaspoon fresh ground pepper
- 1/2 cup slivered almond

Preparation:
Preheat oven to 350 degrees F. Prepare pasta according to package directions.

Melt 2 tablespoons butter in skillet over medium-high heat; add mushrooms and sauté for 4 to 5 minutes.

Stir together mushrooms, chicken, 1/2 cup of the Parmesan cheese, and next six ingredients. Stir in pasta. Spoon mixture into a lightly greased 11x7-inch baking pan. Sprinkle with almonds and remaining 1/2 cup of the Parmesan cheese.

Bake at 350 degrees F. for 40 minutes or until bubbly.

Note: The dish can be made earlier in the day and reheated. It also freezes well.

The Seduction Dinner
Sara Paretsky

Many years ago, when the man I eventually married and I were falling in love, he took me out for wonderful dinners. I decided to learn to cook so that I could create a dinner for him. I think the meal that made him decide that he wanted to stay with me was a mushroom Gruyère omelette.

For many years Courtenay begged for a reprise of this meal, but I had discovered fat, cholesterol and vegetables and it wasn't until our 30th anniversary that I finally acceded to his pleas.

Note: Measurements are approximate as I make up them up as I go. Quantity is for two people, increase if necessary.

Omelette:

There are three steps to this recipe:
1) The Gruyère sauce
2) Sautéed mushrooms
3) Cooking the eggs

The Sauce:
  Butter
  Flour (I get best results with a bleached, all-purpose flour, but if you're experienced with unbleached or other flours, please use those)
  Gruyère, or any other cheese that melts well such as Comté.
  Milk (While milk produces the best results, but you can use skim. Skim milk takes much longer to thicken a sauce than whole.)
  Salt
  Dry Mustard

COOKING WITH CRIMESPREE

Preparation:
In a heavy sauce pan melt 2 tablespoons of butter over low heat (note: butter burns very quickly). Add 2 tablespoons flour to the melted butter and cook over low heat, stirring constantly for 2 minutes. Add a pinch of salt, and a pinch of dry mustard. Add 1 1/2 cups of cold milk and increase the heat to medium heat. Continue to stir constantly, making sure that all of the flour paste in the pan mixes in with the milk. Continue to stir until the sauce thickens, with lava like bubbles beginning to appear in it. Please note: if you let the milk mixture boil you must throw out the sauce and start over as it will never thicken, so you must keep stirring.) Remove from heat and add 1/3 to 1/2 cup of grated or chopped cheese, to taste. Set aside.

Mushrooms:
There are many varieties of mushrooms, but brown, button, or shitakes seem to make better omelettes than portabellos, oysters, or morels. However, you should be guided by your own taste.
Slice a lot of mushrooms. I usually use about 10 for 2 people.
Sautee in melted butter until brown, usually about 2-4 minutes.
Remove the mushrooms from the pan. Set aside.

Omelette:
Turn on broiler to medium heat with oven shelf 6 inches from heat source.
2 eggs per person is my recipe, but you can use more or fewer to taste.
Break eggs into a bowl, whip vigorously with about 2 teaspoons water.
Heat 1 tablespoon olive oil in a small skillet. This takes about 20 second, olive oil scorches at low heat. Add the eggs and tilt pan from side to side so that they spread across the whole skillet. Gently lift the edges of the eggs so that raw egg runs underneath. When the eggs are almost cooked turn off the heat. Layer the mushrooms uniformly across the eggs, pour the sauce over the mushrooms. Place the skillet under the broiler

and heat until the sauce turns golden brown, about 1 to 3 minutes.

Serve with a green salad and your favorite wine. I always use Chateau-Neuf-Du-Pape.

Fettuccini Alfredo, Puzzle Lady Style
Parnell Hall

Cora Felton, the Puzzle Lady, is as bad at cooking as she is at solving crossword puzzles, and she can't solve them at all. (Cora is the Milli Vanilli of the crossword puzzle set. Her niece, Sherry, constructs the Puzzle Lady puzzles for her.) Nonetheless, she has a few surefire recipes. I am happy to include one here:

Preparation:
1) Dump one box fettuccini in boiling water. Leave on stove.
2) Melt cheese. (Parmesan, Romano, cheddar, Swiss, American, or Cheez Whiz)
3) Add milk.
4) Add cream cheese , cottage cheese, or Miracle Whip
5) Pour in salt.
6) Add butter.
7) Add more butter.
8) Combine fettuccini and cheese mixture
9) Taste.
10) Pour fettuccini and cheese mixture into garbage.
11) Place frozen fettuccini dinner in microwave.
12) Zap

Feeds at least one.

Muskrat Fricassee
From Gary Phillips

This recipe is from a cookbook that belonged to my Aunt Margaret who passed away at 96 this past Christmas.

This is an important advisory in the game section of the book from where this recipe comes.

Removal of Shot Area
Some hunters insist that game flesh which is permeated with shot has a better flavor than that which has not been shot. However, most authorities on cooking and dressing game will not concur with this opinion. The mangled holes where shot enters the carcass or "blood shot" areas are unsightly in either the raw or cooked meat and these areas deteriorate and develop off-flavors rapidly. The presence of shot in the cooked meat also makes it unpleasant and even rather hazardous to eat. Hair and feathers are carried into the flesh with the shot and if not removed, they greatly reduce the appetite appeal of the meat.

Whenever possible, therefore, the shot area and any feathers or hair should be removed immediately after bleeding with a sharp pointed knife, and any clotted blood should be squeezed out. With game birds, however, that do not have the feathers removed at once, it is not possible to remove all the shot. As the birds are eviscerated, some of the shot that may have traveled into the body cavity or have broken bones may be discovered and removed. The remaining shot wounds must wait until the feathers or skin are removed. When game is shot up badly, it is usually a waste of time to try to bring it to a state of edibility. It is possible to soak it in salt water long enough to drain out most of the clotted blood, but it also draws out much of the fine flavor.

Muskrat Fricassee

Ingredients:
1 dressed muskrat, 1 to 1 1/2 pounds
1/4 teaspoon pepper
1 tablespoon salt
1/16 teaspoon red pepper
1 quart water
1/4 cup shortening
1/4 cup flour paprika
2 teaspoons salt
1 large onion, sliced (1 cup)
3/4 cup water

Preparation:
Wipe muskrat with damp cloth, pick off any hair. Separate hind from four quarters by cutting across back and just below ribs. Fit into a glass or enamel bowl. Add salt and water to cover. Cover and place in refrigerator overnight. Next day, drain off salt water and rinse muskrat thoroughly in clear water. Drain well. Cut in serving pieces (p. 982). Place flour, salt, pepper, and red pepper in a clean paper bag. Place a few pieces of muskrat at a time in the bag and shake to coat well. Heat shortening in heavy skillet and brown pieces slowly on all sides over medium heat. Sprinkle the browned surface with paprika. Push the muskrat to one side and add onion. Allow to cook until onion is slightly yellow and transparent. Add 1/2 cup water, reduce heat, cover and simmer gently until tender, about 20 to 30 minutes, adding the remaining water as needed. Serve on hot platter with the gravy poured over the top. 2 to 3 servings.

Meta Given's Modern Encyclopedia of Cooking, J. G. Ferguson and Associates, Chicago, First published 1947, 1952 edition—5 printings that year totaling some 151,000 copies

Roast Garlic Mustard Monkfish
Scott Phillips

This started not as a proper recipe but as a very basic set of instructions on roasting monkfish in the New York Times food section a few years back. My version is way better, although it may ruin your baking dish (you've been warned, sometimes this method gunks up the sides of a dish with some solid black stuff that JUST WON'T COME OFF.)

Ingredients:
  12-16 ounces monkfish filet
  1 or 2 heads of garlic, cut into slivers
  Salt and pepper
  Pimenton (aka smoked spanish paprika, or just paprika)
  Dijon mustard (or honey Dijon)
  Dry white wine

Preparation:
Preheat oven to F 475.
Grease up a baking dish with extra virgin olive oil.
Sprinkle salt, pepper and pimenton over the monkfish, then coat it with the mustard.
Put the monkfish into the dish.
Roast it for 15-20 minutes.
Toward the end of the roasting heat up whatever you like to use for sauces—saucepan, skillet, don't matter.
The monkfish should leave a fair amount of juice in your dish. Once you've plated the monkfish, pour the liquid into the hot saucepan (or whatever), quickly followed by a good splash of the wine. It should boil down pretty quickly, and when it gets to be pretty think and viscous pour it onto the fish.

Serves two, or three if one of them's not too hungry.

Mama Rose's Spaghetti Sauce
Robert J. Randisi

Ingredients:
  1 pound can crushed tomatoes
  1 small whole tomato diced
  1 8-ounce can tomato sauce
  1 teaspoon oregano
  2 cloves garlic
  1/2 teaspoon pepper
  5 basil leaves

Preparation:
Grind seasoning together. Heat 1 Tablespoon of oil in pan and sauté seasonings.
  Pour tomatoes in pot. Add 1/2 cup water and seasonings. Simmer for 2 hours.

Pasta on a Deadline
Hank Phillippi Ryan

I always make this on nights when I get home late and still want to come up with a delicious dinner that's quick and easy. The recipe has just a few ingredients—the key is a little parallel processing to make sure all the elements are ready at the same time.

It's one of those recipes where you think you know what it's going to taste like—but it doesn't ! The total of the hot peppers and the garlic and the cheese is more than the sum of the parts!

Ingredients:
  Your favorite pasta (Enough for two people.)
  Penne works well, so does farfalle. Short pasta works better than long pasta.
  Water for cooking pasta
  1 tablespoon chopped garlic
  1/4 cup or a little more olive oil
  1/4 teaspoon red pepper flakes
  1/4 cup or more bread crumbs
  1 bunch broccoli rabe, chopped smallish
  Grated Parmesan cheese (the best quality you can find)
  Salt and pepper to taste

Instructions:
1. Put uncooked pasta in boiling water
2. Put olive oil, garlic, and red pepper flakes in a small bowl, and put in the microwave. (I know you'll wonder if you really need the red pepper flakes—you do!)
3. When pasta is two minutes from done, cook oil mixture in microwave for one and a half minutes on reheat.
4. At essentially the same time, add the chopped broccoli rabe to the cooking pasta.

5. Take the oil mixture out of the microwave, and mix in the bread crumbs to make a paste. The consistency should be more oily than stiff, so add bread crumbs gradually.

6. When the pasta is done, the broccoli will be done. Drain the pasta/broccoli and return to hot pan.

7. Quickly add the oil bread crumb mixture and stir to combine.

8. Serve instantly with grated cheese and salt and pepper. (You don't want this to get cold!)

I've used regular broccoli, and also chopped spinach instead of broccoli rabe—and it still works perfectly. The peppery flavor of the rabe is a nice addition, though. Sometimes I add hot grilled corn kernels at the same time as the oil mixture.

You can also heat the oil mixture in a sauce pan...the key is, you're just heating the oil, not cooking it.

Grown-Up Fish Sticks and Fries
Marcus Sakey

I grew up with a strict Sunday tradition. No, not that one; in my household, Sunday afternoon was about fish sticks, fries, and *Star Trek* reruns on channel 20. Now that we have *Battlestar Galactica*, I figured I'd update the recipe as well.

Fish Sticks
    Catfish fillets
    Milk
    Corn meal
    Chipotle powder
    Sugar
    Salt
    Bacon grease or butter
    Lemon

Fries
    Vegetable oil
    Unpeeled red skin potatoes
    Fresh rosemary sprigs
    Salt

Fish Sticks
Wash the catfish and cut into strips against the grain. Soak in milk and then dredge them in a mix of corn meal, chipotle, salt, and sugar (to your taste; I tend to go heavy on the chipotle and salt). Melt a good quantity of bacon grease or butter in a heavy-bottomed pan over medium-high. When it's almost smoking, put the fish sticks in. Let cook for 2 minutes, flip them, and give them another couple of minutes.

Fries

Fill a tall sauce pan about 2.5 inches deep with cooking oil on medium-high. Matchstick the potatoes and squeeze to remove excess water. Put them in the oil. After about ten minutes, strip the rosemary needles from the twigs and put the needles in the oil. Cook until golden brown, then drain on paper towels. Pour on salt while they're still wet. Lots of salt.

Serve fish sticks and fries together with lemon wedges. No fucking ketchup; if you must dip these fries in something, go with mayonnaise. In the summer, pair with a hoppy IPA (I like Jolly Pumpkin's E.S. Bam); in the winter, with a rich stout (Victory's Storm King).

Chicken Enchiladas to Die For
L.J. Sellers

As busy crime fiction author—who's released 12 books in the last 6 years—I barely have time to cook. But whenever my extended family gets together, they always want my Chicken Enchiladas to Die For. And who can say no to family? No one has ever actually killed anyone over this delicious casserole dish, but my sons have almost come to blows over the last serving. And this dish is guaranteed to make you popular at potlucks.

Ingredients:
    3 large chicken breasts, baked and diced
    1 pint of light sour cream
    1 can of cream of chicken soup
    1 small can of diced green chilies
    2 cups of grated sharp cheddar cheese
    10 or so tortillas (flour or white corn)
    Salt and pepper to taste

Preparation:
This dish is a favorite at family potlucks and easy to make. First, bake and dice the chicken breasts. While they're cooking, mix together everything but the tortillas and chicken. Lightly grease/spray an oven dish like a cake pan. Roll up a portion of the diced chicken with a tablespoon of the sauce mixture in each tortilla. When the pan is filled, cover the enchiladas with the rest of the sauce and bake at 350 for about 25 minutes. Then help yourself to a large portion because there won't be any leftovers.

L.J. Sellers writes the bestselling Detective Jackson mystery series—a two-time Readers Favorite Award winner—as well as provocative standalone thrillers. Her novels have been highly praised by reviewers, and her Jackson books are the highest-rated crime fiction on Amazon. L.J. resides in Eugene, Oregon where her novels are set and is an award-winning journalist who earned the Grand Neal. When not plotting murders, she enjoys standup comedy, cycling, social networking, and attending mystery conferences. She's also been known to jump out of airplanes.

Zipper Lock Salmon Ceviche
Kieran Shea

Ingredients:
  Juice of 1 lime
  Juice of 1 lemon
  Juice of 1 orange
  Zest of half a lemon
  1 small jalapeño pepper (seeded and finely diced)
  4 fresh chives (fine dice)
  1 small handful of well rinsed cilantro leaves (20 or so) chopped
  1 tablespoon of cilantro stems (fine dice)
  1 medium-sized jicama, peeled and julienned into 1-inch thin strips
  1 medium-sized shallot, peeled and cut into fine slices
  1 twelve ounce salmon filet, skinless, pin bones and dark oily meat removed, cut (small dice)
  1 orange sectioned, with rind and white pith removed
  1 large plum tomato (seeded and diced small)
  4 tablespoons of high quality extra virgin olive oil
  Sea salt and ground fresh black pepper to taste
  1 baguette

Tools:
  1 sharp chef's knife and a large 1/2 gallon zipper seal plastic bag

Method:
"Prep" all ingredients but do not combine as ceviche is practically a one-step marinade. When everything is ready ahead of time all you need to do is just combine it all together and zing! You're a hero and back partying with your impressed guests.

Cut all your vegetables, fruit, etc. and reserve and chill until you are ready to go, dicing your salmon filet last. Squeeze and combine your juices and combine the rest of the ingredients in the 1/2 gallon plastic bag, seasoning the contents with sea salt and ground pepper. Seal the bag. Let the combined ingredients rest refrigerated for about ten minutes, gently turning and giving the bag a squeeze a couple of times so things get to know each other. When the salmon is slightly opaque (again about ten minutes) it's ready. Empty the ceviche contents into a bowl and garnish with some extra diced tomato. Serve with a basket of sliced, warm baguette rounds. Spoon ceviche onto a round and enjoy.

A serial re-inventor of identity, Kieran Shea finished at the top of his class in culinary school and owned a maritime catering concern for almost seven years. His crime fiction chops have landed him in nasty places like Ellery Queen Mystery Magazine and Plots With Guns.

Chicken Tacos
Anthony Neil Smith

Ingredients:
  Boneless chicken breasts
  A jar of salsa
  A packet of taco seasoning
  Cheese
  Tortillas
  Beer
  A crock pot.

Preparation:
Place chicken, salsa, and taco seasoning in crock pot. Cover. Cook on low for, like, twelve days (or seven hours).

While they cook, go to work, or write something, or masturbate, or (if luckier) have sex with someone, watch TV, mail bills, browse Rhapsody and wonder why the hell the kids are listening to such crap these days, call your mother, do your laundry, browse some more because you saw an ad for a new Jeep and you wanted to see how cheap you could get it for, but then you give up and just browse to find those photos of Brittany sans underpants.

You can have a beer while doing any of this.

When done, shred chicken with a couple of forks, let it cook another two days (or half an hour).

Heat tortilla (if you can't figure out how, you should've stopped reading this a long time ago).

Put cheese on tortilla. Put tacofied chicken on tortilla. Fold till it looks like a taco.

Eat it. Then drink beer to help ease the burn you just gave the roof of your mouth.

(You should also heat and eat refried beans. The whole goddamned can.)

COOKING WITH CRIMESPREE

Anthony Neil Smith is the former editor of Plots With Guns *and the Author of* Psychosomatic *and* Drummer. *He is sharing with us his recipe for Chicken Tacos.*

Bacalao (cod fish)
Steven Torres

Bacalao was once a staple of the Puerto Rican table (probably still is in many homes) and remains comfort food for many.

But... If you use salted cod fish, you need to give yourself a day or two head start as you'll be getting the salt out through a half dozen repeated soakings.

Ingredients
- 1 pound of salted cod fish
- 1/4 cup of olive oil
- 6-10 garlic cloves
- 1 medium to large onion
- 2 red bell peppers
- 2-3 tomatoes
- 1-2 medium potatoes
- 1/4 teaspoon paprika

Recipe (easy):
Shred the fish, not too finely
Sauté in olive oil with some grated/minced garlic and onions until soft—don't skimp on the oil
Serve with boiled breadfruit (pana), malanga (if you can get it) and yautia.

Recipe (harder):
Shred the fish, not too finely
Sauté grated/minced garlic and chopped onions in olive oil over medium heat until soft—don't skimp on the oil
Add red peppers (hot peppers if you like that sort of thing)
A small amount of paprika (1/4 teaspoon)
A large amount of red tomatoes (1 pound, diced)

A small amount of boiled and diced potato to thicken the sauce you're making

Everything into the blender for a quick puree, then back into the pan to add the cod fish

Almost no chance you'll need salt, but that's up to you

This can be served as an appetizer—with tear breads or crackers, for instance.

Slow Cooker Pork
Bryan VanMeter

Ingredients:
  3-4 pounds pork roast
  1 tablespoon thyme
  1 teaspoons paprika
  2 tablespoons oregano
  Salt
  Pepper
  1 medium onion diced

Preparation:
Put everything into a slow cooker on high for 5-6 hours. Pork will begin to fall apart when done. Serve over long grain rice

Note: this is one of my favorite recipes for coming home from a long day at work. The onions totally dissolve and creates an amazing sauce for the pork

Pate du Chateau Blanc
Elaine Viets

I'm best known for burning boil-in-the-bag lima beans, but I make a pate like no other. When you need recreational calories, cholesterol, and fat, serve this recipe. Good is not the word for Pate du Chateau Blanc. That's White Castle Pate. To make belly bombers for the bon vivant, you grind them in a blender and bake them with bacon. Then you slather the sliders with sour cream. It's murder on the arteries, but you only live once. This recipe was originally published in the Columbus, Ohio, Dispatch.

Take 15 White Castle hamburgers with pickle and onion and buns. Blend the burgers in a blender, three at a time, scraping the sides and adding water as needed for blending. Pour into a lightly buttered loaf pan. If desired, lay raw bacon slices in the pan first. Bake at 325 degrees for 45 minutes. Remove from pan and cool. Serve with a mixture of sour cream, yogurt and chopped parsley. Garnish with additional parsley, as desired.

NOTE: Be sure to add the water BEFORE you start blending the burgers. I burnt out a blender when I forgot to do this.

Elaine Viets. author of Catnapped!, *A Dead-End Job Mystery*

Moroccan Lamb with Prunes and Ginger
Martyn Waites

This is a gorgeous dish, one of my favourites. I've just moved into a new house and we're decorating it with a Moroccan theme so it was only a matter of time before I started on the food. I think this is an authentic recipe even though it doesn't involve any preserved lemons which most Moroccan food does. I love the way they mix savoury things with sweet ones too.

Before I start, I should say that the ingredients are right but don't hold onto the quantities as gospel. Every time I make this I vary it depending on what mood I'm in and what I've got to hand. But here goes.

For six people.

Ingredients:
- At least six lamb steaks. Or you could use chops (but there's not as much meat on them) or diced or cubed lamb but whatever you do, make sure there's enough for six.
- One packet of dried prunes. The kind you get in foil packages from health food stores are the best. They're still really moist.
- At least one tablespoonful of fresh grated ginger. Or more if you like. More is good.
- One onion
- A couple of cloves of garlic
- One large red pepper
- At least one tablespoon of cinnamon
- At least one tablespoon of tumeric
- Salt and pepper
- A big spoonful of clear honey
- An optional tablespoonful of cumin

COOKING WITH CRIMESPREE

Some oil
Some water
Couscous—at least a cupful per person
Raisins
Almonds
Dried apricots
Dash of cumin
Dash of paprika
A bottle of red wine (I find a rich Merlot good for this)

Some music—I'd recommend Drive By Truckers, Flaming Lips or some old Talking Heads but whatever moves you

Method:
I always think there are only two methods of cooking lamb. Either slow cook it to buggery so it's beautifully tender or chuck it in the pan, brown it slightly and serve it so it's so pink in the middle a good vet could get it on its feet again. This recipe goes for the former.

Stick the CD in the player as loud as you can tolerate it. Open the red wine, pour yourself a generous glassful. None of this is to go into the food, it's to go into the chef. Get the mood right before you start.

Pour the oil in a frying pan, heat, then brown the lamb. It doesn't have to be done all the way through, just browned.

Slice the onion and crush the garlic. Don't crush it with a garlic crusher, it loses the taste that way. Instead do it the proper way with the flat of a blade, then chopping what's been crushed. Put some oil in another pan, fry the onions and garlic.

Chop the pepper. Put it in with the onions and garlic.

When the meat is browned, put it in the pan with the onions, pepper and garlic. Cook for a bit. Then slice the prunes in half, removing the stones. Keep the stones because you can play 'Tinker tailor' to pass the time while it's cooking later. Put the prunes in with the lamb, onions and garlic, give a little stir.

Have another glass of wine.

Add the ginger, cinnamon, tumeric and a little salt and pepper if it's needed. Give it a stir. Pour some water over this and cook until the water's boiling. The turn the heat down and cover it with the lid. Leave it to simmer for about an hour.

While that's doing its thing, chop the apricots and almonds in a bowl and mix them together with the raisins. Add the paprika and cumin to taste. I love cumin so I whack a load in.

Change the CD for something a bit more mellow. Sit down, have another glass of wine, read a book. I'd recommend one of mine.

After an hour or so, check on the meat, see how it's doing. The sauce should have reduced a bit. If it hasn't, take the lid of and let the steam rise. Put in the honey, stirring it in.

Boil a panful of water, put the couscous in a streamer and steam it until it's fluffed up. Another way of doing it is to put it in a bowl with a large knob of butter and pour the water directly on to it. It should tell you on the packet how much you need. Let it stands until it's fluffed out then add the chopped fruit, nuts and spices. Stir.

It should be ready to serve. For that authentic ethnic feel, serve it into bowls that are large and heavy and have child-style drawings of primary coloured flowers on the side.

Serve with wine and friends. And a green salad dressed in lemon juice and oil.

Eat, enjoy and bask in the compliments.

Chicken with Potatoes, Prunes and Pomegranate Molasses
Martyn Waites

This is a recipe I nicked from the great Yotam Ottolenghi. I tried it once and it immediately made its way into my (somewhat limited, admittedly) repertoire. It's wonderful for two reasons: It tastes gorgeous—really gorgeous—and it's so easy to make. And I mean SO easy. It's particularly good in autumn and winter, especially when you're on a deadline and you haven't got time to faff about. Try it. You'll thank me for it. Honestly. It should feed about four people.

Ingredients:
- 8 whole chicken legs (thighs and drumsticks), about 2kg in all
- 16 medium charlotte potatoes (about 800g)
- 3 large onions, peeled and quartered
- 120g of pitted prunes
- 30g of grated fresh ginger
- 100ml of soy sauce
- 90 ml pomegranate molasses
- 1 tablespoon maple syrup
- 120g sweet mango chutney
- 1/2 teaspoons whole black peppercorns
- 20g oregano sprigs plus a few picked leaves to garnish

Preparation:
Heat the oven to 200c/390f/gas mark 6. Throw all the ingredients into a bowl, mix together, then tip into a large casserole dish. Cover with foil or a lid and bake for 10 minutes. Lower the heat to 180c/350f/gas mark 4 and cook for 2 hours, stirring every now and then.

And that's it. Told you it was easy.

When it's ready, remove the dish from the oven, stir once again, recover and set it aside for about 15 minutes to rest and allow the flavours to mingle. Throw a few oregano leaves on as garnish, serve it with some greens and chunks of expensive artisan bread (that you can pass off as your own) to mop up the juices.

Oyster Dressing
Dave Wellington

Ingredients:
- 4 ounces oysters, shucked and cleaned
- 1 pound breadcrumbs
- 1/2 stick butter
- 8 ounces heavy cream
- Salt and pepper

Preparation:

This is a dish that was actually served at the first Thanksgiving, and it was a favorite of my grandparents' generation. In my youth my mother would make it every year, but eventually she stopped when she realized my sisters wouldn't eat it. I enjoy it so much I made her tell me how it was done so the recipe wouldn't just disappear.

Preheat oven to 375 degrees. Cut the oysters to the desired size; note they can be chewy unless you really mince them. In a casserole dish, put down a bottom layer of breadcrumbs and pats of butter. Add salt and pepper to taste. Place oysters on top, then another layer of breadcrumbs and butter, salt, and pepper. Pour all of the cream and any remaining oyster liquid over top, thoroughly drenching the dish. Bake for 20 minutes, or until dressing reaches desired consistency—similar to very creamy mashed potatoes. Serve piping hot.

Note that this dish can be cooked alongside a roast or a turkey as desired; it will not burn, though it may dry out if left in too long. It is not safe to cook this dressing inside a turkey.

Cereal Killer Chicken
Jeri Westerson

I reworked this recipe from an old childhood one. It's definitely my favorite way to cook chicken. You can also do this for skinless chicken breasts, use low sodium soy sauce and wheat germ instead of cereal to cut down on the fat and up the fiber. And it's great cold for a picnic. I would murder for a piece right now! This is the kind of recipe that it wonderful for the busy writer because once it's assembled, it just goes in the oven and you forget about it for an hour. Believe me, I cook it all the time while I'm working at home.

Ingredients:
 1 chicken, cut into pieces
 1/2 cup soy sauce
 1 cup corn flakes, flattened into crumbs
 2 tablespoons flour
 Salt, pepper, garlic powder, onion powder, sage, thyme, rosemary
 Cooking spray

Preparation:
Take pieces of chicken and marinate for an hour or two in soy sauce. Keep refrigerated.

In the meantime, assemble the coating. Put corn flakes in a Ziploc bag, making sure the lock is open just enough to allow the expulsion of air. Get a rolling pin and roll over it until flakes become crumbs. Add flour and spices and shake to mix.

Once chicken has marinated, put into Ziploc, two pieces at a time, and shake the coating on.

Spray baking sheet with cooking spray. Arrange chicken pieces on pan and bake in a 425 degree oven for 1 hour and 10 minutes. Check temperature with meat thermometer (should read 165 degrees) for doneness. Great hot or cold.

L.A. native and award-winning author Jeri Westerson writes the critically acclaimed Crispin Guest Medieval Noir novels. Her protagonist is a disgraced knight turned detective, plying his PI trade on the mean streets of fourteenth century London. Jeri is president of the southern California chapter of MWA, a member of the Historical Novel Society, Science Fiction and Fantasy Writers of America, and Sisters in Crime. www.JeriWesterson.com

Olive Cream Pasta
Kate White

I love traveling for all the obvious reasons—the pure bliss of being someplace new and exciting, all the sights to be seen and discoveries to be made, and of course the amazing food you can encounter both from smart planning and a bit of sheer luck. But there's another crazy reason I love to take off for parts unknown. I do some of my best mystery writing when I'm in a new location, particularly if it's over 80 degrees out.

I have no freaking clue why this is. Maybe it's simply because my brain gets recharged in a fresh environment or the mysteriousness of the new surroundings make me think, well, mysteriously. The bottom line is that I never go on vacation without my laptop—and I try to write for about three hours each morning.

The recipe below is one I picked up on my third trip to Provence with my husband. We were staying at a wonderful old hotel in the middle of a vineyard, and though the food (included in the price) was amazing, the choices were fairly limited. One day at lunch we realized that the only thing we both could handle from the list of three entrees—unless we suddenly became fans of bunny rabbit or sweetbreads, and that wasn't about to happen—was a very basic-sounding pasta dish. According to the description on the menu, it seemed to be made with what we thought was mostly olive oil. We worried a little grouchily that we would soon feel hungry again.

Well that didn't happen. The pasta dish was divine, one of the dreamiest I've ever eaten. I took a chance and asked the waitress how it was made, knowing that restaurant staff rarely reveal a recipe, but this chatty waitress spilled the beans (or really olives, I should say), and she also showed me where in the hotel boutique I could buy the secret ingredient.

Because she wasn't on the cooking staff, she only knew the ingredients not the proportions so I had to do a bit of guessing on those. You can fiddle with this as you want. You almost can't go wrong.

Ingredients:
- 4.5-ounce jar of green olive tapenade (or "cream"). I use La Favorita Crema di Olive Verdi, which the hotel sold, and which I now order on Amazon.
- 1/4 to 1/2 cup of heavy cream, heated to almost boiling.
- 3 tablespoons or so of extra virgin olive oil
- 1/4 to 1/2 cup of Parmesan cheese
- Salt and pepper to taste

Directions:
Empty the jar of olive tapenade into a pasta bowl. Cook a box of penne or farfalle according to directions. Drain and add to the bowl. Pour on some of the warmed heavy cream and a splash of olive oil and mix until the sauce coats the pasta. Now toss in the cheese and mix again. If the results are too clumpy, add more cream and a bit more olive oil. Season to taste.

This makes a nice lunch or a first course for dinner, as long as the main dish isn't too rich. When I eat this dish it always brings back memories of summer in Provence, as well as the mystery I worked on each morning in dappled light near a cluster of olive trees.

Kate White, the former editor-in-chief of Cosmo, *is the* New York Times *best-selling author of the Bailey Weggins mystery series and three stand-alone novels of suspense,* Hush, The Sixes, *and* Eyes on You.

Flank Steak Recipe
Benjamin Whitmer

Ingredients:
    Flank steak, as much as you can afford
    Soy sauce, enough to soak half of the flank steak
    Lemon juice, enough to soak the other half

Steps:
Start in the evening. Mix enough soy sauce and lemon juice to float the flank steak you purchased. And I mean float. Don't try to get fancy and just coat it or something stupid. And don't worry too much about the ratio between lemon juice and soy sauce. Try to keep it even, but it's forgiving.

Pour the soy sauce and lemon juice into a container with plenty of room for the flank steak to float. This can run from a Tupperware tub to a garbage can.

Put the container in the fridge. This will take more work with a garbage can than with a Tupperware container.

Take a walk in any direction. Get out of the house, for Chrissake. All you do is stare at the walls, and it's not healthy.

Try not to think about the way her hair smells. Because that's weird, and you're already weird enough.

When you do think about how her hair smells, start walking back. There ain't no point in walking after that, because your mind won't process anything but her.

Do a little cleaning. Nothing big. Maybe vacuum. It's been a while since you've done that.

When the vacuum cleaner starts smoking, take out your clip knife and cut her hair off the roller.

There's no point in keeping her hair. It doesn't even smell like her anymore, it smells like the vacuum cleaner.

Make a can of soup for dinner. Peel the lid back half way and use your Leatherman to hold it over the burner so you don't need a pan.

Cut your finger on the lid trying peel the lid back. Wipe the blood on the cupboards instead of getting a band-aid. Eat the soup with a fork.

Don't drink. Drinking won't make anything better, I can promise you that.

You're tired. You can't sleep. Try to read something tough so it knocks you out. Fail. Try to read something easy until you realize you can't do that, neither.

Drink NyQuil.

Wake up to that pigeon outside your window that starts cooing every morning. Remember the times when it woke the two of you up together? Check your cell phone to see if she emailed or called yet.

She hasn't.

Search your gun cabinet for something that would kill the pigeon without making too much noise. A pellet gun if you have one. Hemingway used to kill pigeons when he was broke and feed them to his family. You read that somewhere. Also notice that all your real guns are dirty.

Put on some country music and clean your guns. Make sure one of the songs is Josh T. Pearson's, "Woman, When I've Raised Hell You're Gonna Know It."

The guns are clean enough. They're meant to be shot, not coddled. A dinged up and dirty gun is like a dinged up and dirty book. It means it means it's being used. A clean book or gun is useless.

Get to writing. If you write something good enough she'll be impressed. Make sure you write how you feel. Townes Van Zandt once said, "There are only two kinds of songs; there's the blues, and there's zip-a-dee-doo-dah." You write the blues. Punch-a-hole-in-the-goddamn-wall blues.

Check your cellphone again. Still no email or phone call. Fuck that. Put on Billy Joe Shaver's "The Real Deal." That's you, you're the real deal. This novel's gonna put their hearts on the floor and stomp on them. They can't know how you feel.

But maybe you're kind of emotionally retarded. You've heard that before. Think about how if you were better at expressing your feelings and shit, then maybe she'd be calling or emailing.

Fuck that. Your feelings are on the page and in your actions. Anybody who tells you they can talk plainly about feelings is either simple or deluded. You have enough integrity that you won't play those kind of horseshit emotional transactions with people.

Look up the difference between "integrity" and "pathology." Ignore the results.

Listen to "Write Your Own Songs" by Willie Nelson. You are the real deal, and fuck all of 'em if they don't like it. Finish writing and don't look at any of it because it'll make you feel like a fake.

You are a fake. Remember when she thought you were so tough and gentle and smart? She's probably figured out what a joke that is. All you do is sit in your little apartment trying to write a halfass decent book. You don't know shit about anything. She'll go on about this painter or philosopher and that. You can't even follow half of what she says.

But you can throw a knife. Where is that damn thing? Aim for Bertrand Russell. I wonder how many other men can do that, stick a knife in The History of Western Philosophy? Not many.

Check her Facebook page. Nothing new.

Your phone says you've got a text. Check it too quickly. A friend asking what you're doing. Mean to respond, but don't.

Worry about money. Money's always a good, clean worry.

Until you start to wonder if it's because she's getting sick of you always being broke. She can find men who can afford to buy her dinner. You couldn't barely afford the flank steak.

Check her Twitter feed. Nothing new.

More writing. Nobody's gonna get what you're trying to do with it except maybe her. Unless she has you figured out.

Don't drink. Unless it's been almost 24 hours since you started marinating the flank steak. Then walk to the liquor store and buy the best bottle of bourbon you can afford.

Return to the apartment and broil the flank steak. Seven to nine minutes on each side. When it's done, cut it into thin strips against the grain. Scoop half of them into a container for later. Put the rest on a plate. You don't need utensils.

Draw a hot bath and take the flank steak and the bourbon into the bath. Eat it with your hands, and drink the bourbon from the bottle. If it's good enough for Jim Harrison, it's good enough for you.

The phone rings. The caller ID says it's her. Answer.

"I'm sorry," she says, "I was walking and there was no signal. What are you doing?"

"Just working on the novel."

"I'm outside."

When you let her in, make no mention of the steaming bath with steak floating in it, the half-finished bottle of bourbon in your hand, all the food and refrigerator parts you've sat out to make room for the garbage can, the guns and books everywhere, the holes in the wall, the blood on the cupboards, the pile of her chopped up hair on the table, the fact that you're naked and smell like meat, the knife sticking out of the bookcase, or the dead pigeon in the sink, which you've gutted and half-plucked.

She knows you. She doesn't need explanations.

Beef and Guinness Casserole
Kevin Wignall

Ingredients:
  1 pound of lean beef
  4 ounces streaky bacon, diced and crisply fried
  Large onion, chopped
  Clove of garlic, crushed
  Half pint of Guinness
  Oil
  Salt and Pepper
  Butter
  8 ounces Button Mushrooms
  Quarter pint of beef stock
  Bouquet Garni
  Teaspoon of grated nutmeg
  Teaspoon of fresh thyme leaves
  Sprig of parsley
  Bay leaf

Preparation:
Cut the meat into four steaks and season. Heat the oil (directly in the casserole dish or use a pan—I use a pan and transfer to the dish afterwards) and sear the meat on both sides—remove and put to one side. Heat the butter and sauté the onions and mushrooms for five minutes. Put back the meat and add all the other ingredients. Bring to a simmer, cover and cook in a preheated oven (150 C/300F, Gas Mk 3) for about two hours. Remove the bouquet garni and the bay leaf, and thicken slightly using either corn flour or arrowroot slaked in a little water.

The meat should melt in the mouth. Serve with vegetables of your choice and some mustard mash. And how about a bottle of Chateau Musar to wash it down?

Chicken & Dumplings
Victoria Wilcox

I have selected this one as something Doc Holliday would have enjoyed. It's a Southern Son recipe Gone West: Chicken & Dumplings made with tortillas! Yum!

Yield: 12-16 servings

Ingredients:
   1 whole chicken
   3 whole bay leaves
   3 cans cream of chicken soup
   5 ribs celery, washed and trimmed
   1 large onion, peeled
   1 package flour tortillas

Directions:
1. Cook chicken with bay leaves as explained on p. 99. When done, remove the chicken from the water to cool, saving all of the cooked broth. Debone chicken. You may substitute a cooked rotisserie chicken and cut the meat from it, discarding skin and bones. If you do, use canned chicken broth (2 quarts) to replace the liquid from cooking a raw chicken.
2. While chicken is cooling down, cut celery lengthwise into very narrow strips, then chop crosswise into very small pieces. Add to broth. Mince onion and also add to broth. Simmer until tender (onions will turn translucent).
3. Blend soup into broth, using a whisk. From this point, you need to be careful because the soup can settle and burn if you don't watch it.
4. Chop the deboned chicken meat and return it to the pot. Cut tortillas into strips, 1-inch wide and about 2 inches long.

5. Raise the heat, if necessary, to keep the pot boiling. Add tortillas, a few at a time, stirring to let them get individually coated with soup before adding the next bunch. This is more time-consuming than just dumping them all in at once, but it keeps the strips from sticking together. This is when the soup can really start sticking to the bottom and burning if you don't keep it stirred.

6. Once all the tortillas have been added, reduce heat. Salt and pepper to taste. If it seems too thin, add more tortillas (if you have any more), but remember that this will really thicken up as it cools.

Moroccan Chicken and Couscous
Michael Wiley

Serves 2-4

When my fictional Chicago PI Joe Kozmarski isn't working a case and often when he is, he eats well and widely. You might find him with pierogi and kolache at his mom's house, barbequed som moo at the Laotian Café Nhu Hoa, roasted chicken at the table of a corrupt cop, or egg foo young at Tommy Cheng's Chinese Restaurant. But when he has time to cook more than toast and eggs, he makes Moroccan Chicken and Couscous, a meal that tastes as good on a freezing night as on a summer evening. Joe discovered a dish like it in a skinny restaurant called Sala that was squeezed between two fat buildings. The restaurant was there for years and years, and then it was gone, and the fat buildings seemed to swell in and fill the absence. The restaurant is gone, like so much else in Joe's life, but when Joe spoons Moroccan Chicken onto a bed of couscous, he remembers.

Ingredients:
1 cup dried couscous
3 cups chicken broth
1 teaspoon finely ground cumin seed
1 teaspoon finely ground coriander seed
Ground black pepper to taste
Cayenne pepper to taste
Salt to taste
1 large carrot
1/4 cup pine nuts
4 boneless, skinless chicken thighs
2 tablespoons olive oil
1 green zucchini

1 yellow squash
1 teaspoon oregano
1 bunch of fresh coriander
Sour cream

What to do with them:
Put couscous in medium glass bowl, add one cup of hot, lightly-salted chicken broth. Cover and set aside. Add most of cumin, coriander, black pepper, and cayenne pepper (reserving some) to remaining two cups of chicken broth. Simmer.

Chop carrot and add to broth. Cook until firm, then ladle carrot onto plate.

While carrot is cooking, toast pine nuts on a pie tin. Cut chicken thighs into 3/4 cubes. Cut zucchini and yellow squash into medallions. Chop fresh coriander.

Heat olive oil in large frying pan to medium high. Sauté zucchini and yellow squash, seasoning with oregano, salt, and black pepper. Stir until firm and lightly brown. Ladle onto separate plate.

In remaining oil, sauté chicken, seasoning with remaining cumin, coriander, black pepper, and cayenne, stirring until almost done. Add 3/4 cup of remaining chicken broth and all of the chopped carrot. Keep on heat until most of the broth has cooked away and the chicken is done.

Remove from heat. Stir in cooked zucchini and yellow squash. Add fresh coriander to taste.

On dinner plates, make a bed of couscous, and spoon chicken and vegetables onto it. Pour additional broth on top until chicken and couscous mixture is damp. Add fresh coriander, and sprinkle with toasted pine nuts. Put dollop of sour cream on the side.

Michael Wiley writes the Shamus Award-winning Joe Kozmarski PI series and the Daniel Turner thrillers.

DESSERTS

"Life is uncertain. Eat dessert first."
—Ernestine Ulmer

Meet Your Baker: Raspberry Danish
Ellie Alexander

Ingredients:
- 2 packages of yeast
- 1/2 cup warm water
- 1 teaspoon sugar
- 1 cup milk
- 1 teaspoon salt
- 4 tablespoons butter
- 4 cups of flour
- 1/2 cup sugar
- 1 jar raspberry jam

Directions:

Mix the yeast into the warm water and let rise for 10 minutes. While that's rising, melt the butter in the milk. Sift the flour and sugar into a large mixing bowl. Add the yeast, milk and butter to the flour mix and knead until it doesn't stick to the bowl. Cover with a kitchen towel and let it rise for 15 minutes. Grease two 8-inch round cake pans. Divide dough into two balls. Pat into the cake pans. Prick with a fork, cover with the kitchen towel and let rise for 15 minutes. Drizzle with raspberry jam and bake at 425 degrees for 12 minutes. If desired glaze with vanilla frosting (recipe below) as soon as you remove from the oven. Allow to cool before serving. Slice and enjoy!

Frosting:
- 1 stick butter
- 2 cups powdered sugar
- 1 teaspoon vanilla
- 1/4 cup milk

Directions:
Whip butter, add powdered sugar, vanilla and milk. Mix until blended. Drizzle over warm Danish.

Chocolate Hazelnut Torte
Ellie Alexander

Ingredients:
 6 eggs
 3/4 cup sugar
 3/4 cup flour
 1 cup ground hazelnuts (plus 10-15 whole hazelnuts for garnish)
 1/2 teaspoon cream of tartar
 1/2 teaspoon almond extract

Directions:
Separate eggs. Save egg yolks for later. Beat egg whites and cream of tartar until they form soft peaks then add sugar and beat to stiff peaks. In a separate bowl, beat egg yolks until the turn pale yellow. Add almond extract, ground nuts and flour. Fold egg whites into yolk mixture. Pour into spring form pan or two 9-inch round pans. Bake at 350 degrees until set, 25-30 minutes. Allow to cool and slice cakes horizontally into four or six layers. Reserve the best layer for the top of the cake.

Mocha Buttercream Frosting:
 3 sticks of butter
 1 teaspoon instant coffee
 2 eggs
 1 pound confections sugar (powdered sugar)
 4 ounces semi-sweet baking chocolate
 Apricot jam or preserves
 Hazelnuts for garnish

Directions:
Beat eggs and coffee in a heavy-bottom saucepan on medium-low until well mixed. Then stir in sugar, stirring

continually. Heat until hot, but not boiling. Remove from heat, add chocolate and butter while still warm. Cool frosting to room temperature before assembling torte.

    Assemble by frosting each layer and then frost the sides. Leave an extra lip around the top layer or pipe an edge around it. Do not frost top layer. Strain apricot jam or preserves through a sieve. Spread jam on top layer. Garish ring edge of top layer with whole hazelnuts.

Key Lime Tarts
Victoria Allman

Crust:
    1 cup graham crackers
    2 tablespoons sugar
    1/2 cup melted butter

Filling:
    4 egg yolks
    1 can (14 ounces) sweetened condensed milk
    8-12 Key limes, juiced (to make 2/3 cup juice), zest kept from 2 of the limes

Topping:
    1 1/2 cups heavy cream
    1/4 cup confectioner's sugar
    1 teaspoon vanilla

Crust:
    Preheat the oven to 325 degrees

Break up the graham crackers, place in a food processor and process to crumbs. Add the melted butter and sugar and pulse until combined. Press the mixture into the bottom of 3 1/2 inches tart shells, forming an even layer on the bottom. Bake the crusts for 10 minutes. Remove from the oven and cool.

Filling:
In a standing mixer with the wire whisk attachment, whip the egg yolks and lime zest at high speed for 5 minutes until fluffy. Gradually add the condensed milk and continue to whip for 4 minutes until thick. Lower the mixer speed and slowly add the lime juice until incorporated.

Pour the mixture into the crust and bake for 15 minutes, or until the filling has just set. Cool and then refrigerate for 20 minutes.

Topping:
Whip the cream and confectioners' sugar until stiff. Whip in vanilla. Evenly spread the whipped cream on top of the tarts, and place in the freezer for 20 minutes prior to serving.

Serves 8

Victoria Allman, author of Sea Stories of Strong Women. *www.victoriaallman.com*

Gooey Butter Cake
Christy Campbell

Who doesn't like butter, sugar and cream cheese? What is not to love! Best to eat this warm!

This is a 2 step process. First, mix 1 box of yellow cake mix, 1 stick butter (melted), and 1 egg. The mixture will be thick and sticky. Press into a 9x13-inch pan (a glass Pyrex works best).

Next step, 2 eggs, 1 box powdered sugar, and 1 (8 ounces) softened cream cheese. Mix soft cream cheese, 2 eggs, and powder sugar. Spread on top of cake batter in pan. Bake at 350 for 30 to 40 minutes. When it gets golden brown, it is done. The glass pan works well because you can look under to see that the cake is done and will look darker brown. Cool for an hour to let is set up.

Apple Cinnamon Cheesecake
Joelle Charbonneau

Crust:
- 1 cup crushed graham crackers
- 3-4 TB butter
- 3 TB sugar
- 1 teaspoons cinnamon

Cheese mixture:
- 2 packs of cream cheese—softened
- 1/2 cup sugar
- 1 teaspoons vanilla
- 2 eggs

Topping:
- 4 large granny smith apples sliced thin
- 1/3 cup sugar
- 1 teaspoons cinnamon
- 1/2 cup halved pecans

Preparation:
Preheat oven to 350

Mix graham crackers, melted butter, sugar and cinnamon in a bowl. Press mixture into a 9-inch spring pan. Bake for 10 minutes.

Mix cream cheese, sugar and vanilla together. Add eggs one at a time—beat until creamy. Pour mixture on top of crust.

Toss apples, sugar and cinnamon together. Place on top of cheese mixture. Sprinkle pecans on top.

Bake for 70 minutes. Remove from oven and use a knife around the edge. Wait for the cake to cool before releasing the spring pan. Chill before serving. Enjoy!

Raisin Muffins
Clare Donohue

Makes 12 medium or 9 large muffins

Ingredients:
2 cups all-purpose flour
1/2 teaspoons bread soda (level)
1 cup sugar
1/2 stick butter
1 cup raisins
1 egg
1 cup Buttermilk

Preparation:
Preheat oven to 375. Heat the muffin pan slightly then butter and flour pan.
In large bowl, mix the flour and bread soda. Sift well. Add sugar and sift again. Cut up butter into small pieces and work into the dry mixture until it feels like oatmeal. Add raisins and sift again.
In small bowl, whisk the egg. Shake buttermilk then add to egg and whisk. Add to dry ingredients and mix until dough forms. Lift the dough as you mix to aerate.
Spread dough evenly among 12 muffin cups, bake for 20-25 minutes.

Pear Sorbet
J.T. Ellison

One of the things I loved the most in Paris was the dessert sorbets. Pear, in particular, was exquisitely yummy—tart and sweet, smooth on the tongue, freezing cold, perfect to lower body temps on a hot summer day. I set about trying to make the perfect Pear Sorbet, and we've finally come up with an easy, yummy recipe. It's a great light alternative to ice cream, and better for you, too! And you can make this recipe with any fruit and fruit nectar you can find. Peach and mango are delightful.

Ingredients:
- 2 pounds of pears (4-6 depending on size and kind—I like to make this with Anjou pears)
- 1 1/2 cups pear nectar, divided (pear juice works too, just increase your pears by 2 to get the right consistency)
- 3/4 cup sugar
- 1 tablespoon fresh lemon juice
- If you want to get really fancy, a bit of vanilla or lavender will alter the taste ever so slightly

Directions:

Quarter, core, peel, and roughly chop the pears.

Put the chopped pears, 1/2 cup of the pear nectar, and the sugar in a medium saucepan.

Cook, stirring occasionally, until the mixtures comes to a boil.

Reduce heat to maintain a steady simmer and cook, still stirring when you think of it, until the pears are tender and the liquid has thickened a bit, about 10 minutes.

Whirl the mixture in a blender until very smooth. (This is harder to do than it sounds—don't skimp on time. Smoothness makes the end result silky, not grainy.)

Transfer the mixture to a mixing bowl and let it come to room temperature.

Cover and put in the fridge until chilled, usually a few hours (you can speed up this process by putting the pears in a metal mixing bowl, nesting that bowl inside a large bowl filled with ice water, and stirring the mixture until it's chilled).

Stir in the remaining 1 cup of pear nectar and the fresh lemon juice

Freeze in an ice cream maker according to manufacturer's directions.

If you don't have an ice cream maker, transfer to a large metal pan or metal mixing bowl and put in the freezer.

Stir the mixture every 30 minutes or so until it's all frozen.

Once it's all frozen, whip it with electric beaters to lighten the texture, if you like, and then refreeze it before serving.

Killer Peanut Butter Fudge
Jack Getze

Ingredients:
- 2 cups refined sugar
- 3/4 cup whole milk
- 1 teaspoon vanilla extract
- 6 teaspoon gobs of Jif Extra Chunky

Preparation:
Heat milk in large pot, add sugar so each grain gets wet. (It'll burn if you don't.)

On low to medium heat, cook mixture of milk and sugar approximately twenty minutes. My father taught me a test to see if "it's candy yet." Let a drop fall off your stirring spoon into a tall glass of cool water. If the mixture is ready—it's its candy—the mixture will solidify at the bottom of glass. It won't spread out. A tight ball of candy is perfect!

Take off heat and add the vanilla and the peanut butter. Let cool two or three minutes—I like to see the peanut butter melting. Mix and stir vigorously until it starts to harden. Pour out quickly onto flat dish.

Cut into squares. If you couldn't wait long enough and it wasn't quite cooked, you'll have to eat gobs with a spoon.

Blueberry Pie
Sara Gran

Ingredients:
  1 pie shell
  1 package frozen organic blueberries
  A little bit of sugar

Preparation:
Preheat the oven to about 350. Prick the pie shell with a fork a few times, then put it in the oven for about 15 minutes, until it's a little browned. Put the blueberries in the pie shell (you can use all, or just some). Add a little bit of sugar, or omit if desired. Put the pie in the oven and cook until it looks pie-ish. Remove, let cool a few minutes (or as long as you want) and then it's done and you have a pie. Yes, you now have pie. You can use any fruit you like, but I think its best with blueberries.

Actually, I've never made this pie, so I don't know what the hell I'm talking about, but my boyfriend makes it often and I think this is how he does it.

Grandmother's Chocolate Caramel Bars
Andrew Grant

1 pound shortbread (8 ounces flour, 5 ounces butter, 2 ounces sugar)

Make as for shortbread. Press into flat 1-inch tin (rectangular). Bake in preheated oven for 25 minutes at 325F. Leave to cool.

Ingredients:
- 4 ounces butter
- 4 ounces sugar
- 2 tablespoons syrup
- 2 ounces condensed milk

Put into a pan and stir continuously. Bring gently to the boil and boil for exactly 5 minutes. Pour this onto shortbread, and when cool spread with 3 ounces (2 squares) of cooking chocolate.

Strawberry Pizza
Penny Halle

Mix together:
- 1 1/2 cup flour
- 2 sticks of soft butter
- 1/4 cup powdered sugar

Mix and pat on an ungreased pizza pan. Bake at 350 until lightly brown. About 15-20 minutes.

Mix well:
- 1 cup powdered sugar
- 8 ounces room temp cream cheese
- 1/4 teaspoons vanilla

Spread over cooled crust

Cover cream cheese mixture with sliced fresh strawberries. Make your own design. Can add raspberries. Takes about 1 1/2 quarts of berries.

Make or buy a strawberry glaze. Pour over berries and refrigerate 2-4 hours.

Serve in wedges.

Berta's Carrot Cake
Terry Hayes

Ingredients:
- 2 cups unbleached all-purpose flour
- 2 cups granulated sugar
- 2 teaspoons of baking soda
- 2 teaspoons of ground cinnamon
- 1 cup corn oil
- 3 eggs, lightly beaten
- 2 teaspoons of vanilla extract
- 1 1/3 puréed, cooked carrots
- 1 cup chopped walnuts
- 1 cup shredded coconut
- 3/4 cup canned crushed pineapple, drained

Preparation:
Preheat the oven to 350 degrees Fahrenheit. Line a 9x13-inch layer cake pan with waxed paper, and grease the paper.

Sift the flour, sugar, baking soda and cinnamon together in a large bowl. Add the oil, eggs and vanilla and beat well. The fold in the carrots, walnuts, coconut and pineapple. Pour the batter into the prepared pan.

Place it on the middle rack of the oven and bake until the edges have pulled away from the sides of the pan and a toothpick inserted in the center comes out clean, 1 hour.

Cool the cake in the pan for 10 minutes. Then invert it over a cake rack and unmold, remove the waxed paper, and continue to cool for 1 hour.

Frost the top and sides of the cooled cake with cream cheese frosting, and dust the top with confectioner's sugar.

Cream Cheese Frosting (Frosting for a 9x13-inch cake):
    4 ounces cream cheese, at room temperature
    3 tablespoons unsalted butter, at room temperature
    1 1/2 confectioner's sugar
    1/2 teaspoons vanilla extract
    Juice of 1/4 lemon

Cream the cream cheese and butter together in a mixed bowl.

Slowly sift in the confectioner's sugar, and continue beating until fully incorporated (there should be no lumps). Stir in the vanilla and lemon juice.

Mexican Chocolate Icebox Cookies with Dulce de Leche Filling
Tim Hennessy

I would love to pretend that I have any baking skills whatsoever. When pressed to bring desserts I've resorted to dressing up store bought bakery or just simply hiding the packaging. Thankfully, my wife Carrie loves to bake and is pretty great at it.

Here's one of our favorite cookie recipes. The first bite is deceptively sweet and for a moment you're sure you're eating just another cookie. Then the heat kicks in and leaves it's mark on your taste buds and you'll start reaching for another.

Prep: 45 minutes
Chill: 5 hours
Bake: 12 minutes per batch
Cool: 2 minutes per batch
Oven: 325 degrees F

Ingredients:
    3/4 cup butter, softened
    1 cup sugar
    3/4 cup Dutch-processed cocoa powder
    1/2 teaspoon ground cinnamon
    1/4 teaspoon salt
    1/4 teaspoon cayenne pepper
    1 egg
    1 1/2 teaspoons vanilla
    1 1/4 cups all-purpose flour
    1/2 cup dulce de leche

Preparation:

In a large bowl beat butter with an electric mixer on medium to high speed for 30 seconds. Add sugar, cocoa powder, cinnamon, salt, and cayenne pepper. Beat until combined, scraping side of bowl occasionally. Beat in egg and vanilla until combined. Beat in as much of the flour as you can with the mixer. Using a wooden spoon, stir in any remaining flour.

Divide dough in half; cover and chill 1 hour or until dough is easy to handle.

Shape each portion of dough into a roll about 1 3/4 inches in diameter. Wrap rolls in plastic wrap or waxed paper and chill for 4 hours or until firm enough to slice.

Preheat oven to 325 degrees F. Line a cookie sheet with parchment paper. Cut rolls into 1/4 slices. Place slices 1-inch apart on prepared cookie sheets.

Bake for 12 to 14 minutes or until edges are firm. Cool on cookie sheets for 2 minutes. Transfer cookies to wire racks; cool.

Spread dulce de leche on the bottom sides of half the cookie. Top with the remaining cookies, bottom sides down, pressing together lightly to makes sandwiches.

Makes 24 sandwich cookies.

Don't substitute dulce de leche ice cream topping.

To store: Layer sandwich cookies between sheets of waxed paper in an airtight container; cover. Store in refrigerator for up to 3 days. Or freeze unassembled cookies for up to 3 months.

Melt-in-Your-Mouth Ginger Snaps
Sara J. Henry

Ingredients:
  1/2 cup butter (1 stick)
  1/4 cup blackstrap molasses
  1 cup sugar (I use slightly less)
  1 egg
  1/4 teaspoon salt (again, I use slightly less)
  2 teaspoons baking soda
  1 teaspoon cinnamon
  1 teaspoon allspice
  1 teaspoon ground ginger
  2 cups unbleached white flour
  1 to 2 tablespoons additional sugar

Preparation:
Preheat oven to 350 F. Lightly grease cookie sheets—I rub the butter wrapper on them.

Melt butter over low heat. Beat in molasses and a bit less than 1 cup of sugar. Beat the egg by itself in a small bowl and stir into the molasses mixture.

Now stir the dry ingredients together (except the additional sugar) and mix them into the butter-molasses-sugar-egg mixture.

Use your hands (flour them if necessary) to form small balls of dough. Put 1-2 tablespoons sugar on a small plate or bowl, and drop the cookies in them before placing, sugar side up, on the cookie sheet—this provides the crackle.

Bake 12-15 minutes—take out before they are firm—otherwise they can turn into ginger snap bricks. Cool on a rack.

Grandma Judy's Praline Cake
J.A. Jance

Cooking Time: 35 minutes
Prep Time: 20 minutes
Ingredients

For the Cake:
    1 cup dry oatmeal
    1 cup cold water
    1 cup regular white sugar
    1 1/4 cup dark brown sugar
    1 cup vegetable oil
    2 eggs
    1 1/2 cups all-purpose flour
    1 teaspoon baking soda
    1 teaspoon cinnamon
    1/4 teaspoon salt

For the Icing:
    1 stick butter!
    3 tablespoons whole milk
    11/2 cups dark brown sugar
    11/2 cups chopped pecans

Cooking Instructions

For the Cake:
Combine the Oats and Water in a small bowl and set aside.
    Cream the Sugars, Butter, Eggs and Oil in a larger bowl. Make sure all lumps are out of the mixture.
    Add the Oats mixture, Flour, Baking Soda, Cinnamon and Salt. Mix thoroughly.

Grease and flour a 9x13-inch rectangular baking pan or Pyrex pan. Pour in batter.

Bake at 350 for 35 minutes. Check for doneness with a toothpick in the center of the cake.

When done, turn off oven and leave cake in the oven while you make the icing.

For the icing:
In a sauce pan, combine Butter, Milk and Brown Sugar.
Bring to a boil and boil for 1 minute
Add Pecans and mix together off the heat.
Remove cake to stove top and pour hot icing over cake. Spread while hot.

Let icing cool to set and eat cake and icing with a side of Vanilla Ice Cream.

Channeling Estelle's Apple Pie
Ruth Jordan

It's autumn, that glorious time of year when even the most antiseptic of supermarkets take on the remarkable scent of fresh apples. A variety of the red, green, and yellow fruits enough to make any farmer's head spin presents itself. I make pie. In my kitchen it's a tactile experience and a visit of family history. But people seem to like it. The taste is worth the work and for me the work is about the memories of long ago days spent in my Grandmother's Kitchen and Mom's newlywed story.

The Filling:
The key here is Assortment.
You need 12 apples (unless you're anal about coring, then you can cut it to 10).
My current mixture is 4 galas, 2 Fijis, 2 Jonathan, 2 granny smiths and 2 MacIntosh (this last is our unsung hero, breaking down quickly to make a memorable syrup).
Put peeled* apple slices (some thick, some thin) in a large mixing bowl, add 1/4 cup flour, 3 pinches of salt and 1/4 cup of sugar (use more only if your apple assortment is particularly tart) and spices to taste,
Ruth's spice (1 teaspoon cinnamon, 1 pinch ginger, 2 pinches nutmeg). Toss with abandon and set aside to begin fermenting. Now preheat your oven to 375.

*Mom's story, "The pie was beautiful, the crust perfectly browned, syrup oozing through the crust. No one told me I had to peel the apples."

The Crust
A family tradition, the secret to all of my pies. Estelle was my grandmother. A single mother with Irish attitude. I was 7 when

she figured I was old enough to learn how to make basic crust. The kitchen on Utica Street in Clinton N.Y. holds many of my favorite memories but none is better than the day I made my first pie crust. I felt like the secrets of the universe had been released; passed down to me to be preserved for all time. All by a marvelous grandmother, teaching the secrets of the "Faye" crust while drinking Old Milwaukee and smoking Pall Malls.

2 cups flour ("you have to sift the flour 3 times")

1 teaspoon salt ("but make a bowl with your palm, no need to dirty extra utensils")

2 pinches of baking powder ("it's what makes the crust flaky every time")

2/3 cups Lard ("Crisco and Pam have their uses Ruth but the only way to make a pie crust is with lard")

2 to 4 tablespoons of hot water ("the secret to great crust is keeping it as dry as possible. You don't need as much hot water as cold")

Cut lard into dry ingredients with a pastry cutter until mealy. Add water 1 tablespoon at a time, knead the crust (washing hands frequently) until a stiff but pliable dough is created. Separate into two equal size balls of dough.

Spread wax paper on your work surface, sprinkle with flour. Place first ball on paper, flatten with fist. Dust with fine amount of flour, cover with second piece of wax paper and roll out. Peel off top layer of wax paper and flip crust into large pie plate. Remove wax paper. Pour apple mixture into pan. Top with 2 tablespoons of butter.

Spread wax paper on your work surface, sprinkle with flour. Place second ball on paper, flatten with fist. Dust with fine amount of flour, cover with second piece of wax paper and roll out. Peel off top layer of wax paper and place on top of pie. Use fork to vent top crust. Sprinkle with cinnamon sugar. Bake for 50 to 60 minutes keeping an eye on the pie for the last 10 minutes of cooking.

Let cool for 20 minutes. Serve with vanilla ice cream and/or a wedge of sharp cheddar. Simple and full of memories.

Cheesecake
Paul Jordan

Crust
- 1 1/2 cups graham cracker crumbs
- 1/2 stick butter melted
- 2 tablespoons sugar
- 1 teaspoon all-purpose flour

Filling
- 2 pounds (32 ounces) cream cheese room temp.
- 1 cup sugar
- 2 eggs beaten to blend
- 1 teaspoon vanilla extract
- 1 teaspoon almond extract
- 1 can of pie filling (optional)

For crust:
Preheat oven to 350. Combine crumb, melted butter, sugar, and flour in medium bowl and mix thoroughly. Pat mixture into bottom and sides of 10-inch spring form pan. Bake 5 min. Let cool. Turn off oven.

For Filling:
Beat cream cheese, 1 cup sugar, eggs, vanilla, and almond extract at low speed in a large mixing bowl until smooth. Pour into crust. Place in oven: turn temp back to 350. Bake until firm around outer 2 inches and center still loose. About 30 minutes. For best results refrigerate overnight. Pour pie filling over top right before serving.

For Chocolate
- Add 2 tablespoons of coco powder to filling mix
- Add 1 20-ounce package of chocolate chips to filling
- Top with chocolate whipped cream instead of fruit

Gooey Butter Cookies
Matthew McBride

I love to make Gooey Butter Cookies (and by me, I pretty much mean my wife).

It's quick and easy and—if you do it right—they will literally melt in your mouth and dissolve on your tongue. But the key is to watch them cook. So pull up a chair and a deck of cars and play a game of solitaire on the stove.

Ingredients:
 1/2 cup of (softened) butter
 8 ounces of cream cheese
 1/4 teaspoon of vanilla extract
 1/4 cup powdered sugar
 1 box of yellow cake mix
 1 egg

Directions:
Preheat oven to 350 F
Mix the cream cheese and the butter in a bowl with the egg and vanilla. Stir until well blended. Roll into 1-inch balls and then roll the balls in powdered sugar. Place 1-inch apart on a cooking sheet. Bake for 5 to 10 minutes* and eat immediately.

Gooey Butter Cookies are the best when they're, y'know, gooey. This cannot be stressed enough. You'll want them soft, tacky, so you must baby-sit them. Don't wander too far from the kitchen.

Matthew McBride is the author of Frank Sinatra in a Blender *(New Pulp Press). He lives on a farm outside Mount Sterling, Missouri. He has two kids, three dogs, a cat, and a bull. When he's not writing books or causing trouble, he's eating chili.*

Chocolate Zucchini Bread
Erica Ruth Neubauer

Makes 3 loaves.

Ingredients:
- 3 cups flour
- 3 cups sugar
- 1/2 cup cocoa (Dark chocolate!)
- 1 1/2 teaspoons baking powder
- 1 1/2 teaspoons baking soda
- 1 teaspoons salt
- 1/4 teaspoons cinnamon
- 4 eggs
- 1 1/2 cups vegetable oil
- 2 tablespoons butter, melted
- 1 1/2 teaspoons vanilla extract
- 1 1/2 teaspoons almond extract
- 3 cups grated zucchini

Preparation:
In a large bowl, combine the first seven ingredients. Combine the eggs, oil, butter and extracts; mix well. Stir into dry ingredients just until moistened. Fold in zucchini. Pour into three greased and floured 8x4x2 loaf pans. Bake at 350 for 55 to 60 minutes or until a toothpick inserted near the center comes out clean. Cool for 10 minutes. Remove from pan to wire racks.

Pineapple Icing
Marie Nicoll

Ingredients:
- 1/2 cup granulated sugar
- 1/4 cup powdered sugar
- 1 cup grated pineapple
- 1 egg white

Beat together until nice and thick. Then spread on cake or cupcakes in swirls

Chocolate Bars Studded with Walnuts
Neil Plakcy

I don't have plastic chocolate molds so I use square tart pans (sold as individual brownie pans) lined with parchment paper as molds but you can use mini muffin tins or any metal mold as well. The chocolate shrinks slightly when setting so they will slip out of the molds easily.

Ingredients:
   8 ounces semi-sweet good-quality dark chocolate, chopped finely
   3/4 cup toasted walnuts, chopped

Directions:
Preheat oven to 350 degrees.
Place the walnuts on a cookie sheet in a flat layer and bake for 5-7 minutes to toast them.
Remove from oven and cool completely.
Melt 6 ounces chocolate in a bowl set over a pan of barely simmering water.
Once the chocolate is melted, remove the bowl from the pan and add 2 ounces of finely chopped chocolate, stirring constantly to melt it.
Pour a layer of chocolate the molds, then, working quickly, top with walnuts.
Shake the pan slightly to level chocolate.
Put the bars in the refrigerator until firm, five minutes.
Remove from molds and store at room temperature for up to one month...or eat instantly

Readers of my golden retriever mysteries may recall the cafe in the center of Stewart's Crossing, The Chocolate Ear, where my protagonists, Steve Levitan and his golden retriever

Rochester, often visit. The proprietor, Gail Dukowski is like Steve a returnee to Bucks County after a career as a pastry chef in New York. She prepares delicious sandwiches and desserts for her human customers, and always has some fresh-baked biscuits for Rochester, too.

In the first chapter of Whom Dog Hath Joined, Steve and his girlfriend Lili take Rochester with them to the Harvest Fair at the Friends' Meeting in Stewart's Crossing. Gail is there, selling her walnut-studded chocolate bars as an introduction to new customers.

One of the great things about belonging to the Florida chapter of Mystery Writers of America has been meeting and becoming friends with lots of other terrific authors. One of those is yacht chef Victoria Allmann, who has already published two volumes of her foodie adventures on the high seas, Sea Fare: A Chef's Journey Across the Ocean and SEAsoned: A Chef's Journey with her Captain. She was kind enough to develop this recipe for me, for chocolate bars very much like those Gail sells. With only two ingredients, they're easy enough for any home chef to prepare.

Victoria added a note, based on a reader's comment:

Victoria's note: This two-step process of melting chocolate in stages is called tempering the chocolate. For reasons that I don't understand, chocolate gets a white chalky bloom if you melt it straight. Tempering chocolate is what gives it that shiny look of finished chocolates instead of the dull chalky look of raw chocolate out of a package. Like a lot of cooking/baking, there is a science behind it that has to do with molecular structure but I cannot fathom it or explain it, I just know you have to do it ;-)

Lemon Ginger Scones
Linda Richards

When I think about it, all of protagonists in my various series would eat these scones. The version that would come out of Kitty Pangborn's (Death Was in the Blood) Los Angeles (the early 1930s) would feature something less exotic than ginger (though lemon would have been available), but they would have been a rich-feeling treat saved for days when there was a bit of extra butter. Since there are no eggs, though, scones would have been an attainable Depression-era delicacy.

Madeline Carter's (Mad Money, The Next Ex) mom is a tea drinker. Nicole Charles (If It Bleeds) is the child of Scottish immigrants. It's not inconceivable that scones feature in both of these women's diet somehow.

None of that, of course, is why I make them. They are easy. Dependable. Not terribly fussy. And for some reason, they are deeply impressive. Everyone always loves them and when I have friends staying over, I always have to make a double batch because people will take two or three.

Just to be clear, the differences between American biscuits and British scones are important, though their making is similar enough that, at a glance, one can be confused for the other. To confuse things further, biscuits can be sweet and scones can be savory but, in both cases, that is the exception, not the rule. And where biscuits are served as part of a meal, generally at the side, scones are a glorious thing unto themselves, meant to be topped with jam, butter or even heavy cream. They are meant to feel wonderfully rich and decadent and they do. And they are.

The name of this particular recipe is a bit deceiving. These are Lemon Ginger scones because that's what I put in them: Lemon and Ginger. You can replace the lemon and ginger in the recipe below with any number of interesting things including raisins, currents or even chocolate chips or cheese (but please not both at once).

The instructions below call for a food processor. If you don't have one, you can go old school and use a pastry cutter, blending the butter and dry ingredients by hand until the mixture looks like small peas.

Want to do a vegan version? Replace the milk or buttermilk with coconut milk and the butter with a vegan margarine like Earth Balance and—voila!—vegan scones.

Lemon Ginger Scones

Ingredients:
- 1 teaspoon salt
- 1/2 teaspoon baking soda
- 1 1/2 teaspoons baking powder
- 3 tablespoons sugar
- 2 cups all-purpose or unbleached flour
- 1/2 cup COLD butter, cut into 2-inch chunks
- 1 scant cup buttermilk OR 2/3 cup milk and 1/3 cup sour cream
- 1/3 cup chopped crystalized ginger
- 1 tablespoon lemon zest or zested ginger
- Sugar for dusting (optional)

Preparation:
Preheat oven to 350 F.

Place salt, baking soda, baking powder, sugar, flour and butter in the food processor. Pulse briefly as many times as necessary until the butter is incorporated. Ideally it will look like peas in snow, but most modern food processors are so powerful, you go straight to the snow stage. In any case, you want to work with the dough as little as possible to avoid toughness.

Transfer dry ingredients to a mixing bowl. Add raisins, lemon or ginger (if using) and the milk or buttermilk. Using a spatula, stir gently, just until the ingredients are mixed. The dough will be slightly sticky. If the dough seems too wet, add another tablespoon of flour and give it one more stir.

Transfer the dough to a floured surface and knead gently, just until it's well enough incorporated to form into a large ball. Keep in mind that the less you handle the dough, the more tender the scones will be. Flatten the ball until you have a rough circle, about one inch thick. Cut, pie-style, for eight equal triangular-shaped pieces. Place on a parchment-covered baking sheet and sprinkle each piece with the reserved sugar.

Bake in a preheated oven for 20 minutes, or until the scones are golden brown.

Serve with butter or your favorite jams and jellies though they're also pretty great on their own.

Makes eight scones.

Kat's Infamous Spicy Apple Pie
Kat Richardson

Makes one 9-inch deep dish pie.

Ingredients:
- 7 medium or 8 small Granny Smith Apples, pared and sliced (or any appropriate pie apple)
- 2/3 cup granulated sugar (can use 50% brown sugar instead)
- 1/2 cup raisins
- 1/2 coarsely chopped walnuts (optional, or pecans may be substituted)
- 3-4 Tablespoons all-purpose flour
- 1/4 teaspoon salt
- 1 Tablespoon ground cinnamon (preferably very fresh)
- 1 rounded teaspoon ground nutmeg (again, the fresher the better)
- 1 teaspoon ground ginger (1/2 teaspoon fresh grated may be substituted)
- 1/4-1/2 teaspoon ground cayenne pepper (more for "hot" pie, less for "mild")
- 3 Tablespoons lemon juice
- Crust for a 9-inch 2-crust, deep-dish pie (I cheat and buy them ready made, because I suck at crust)
- 1/2 cup bourbon or dark, flavorful rum (optional)
- 1/2 stick of butter (if you use the bourbon/rum)
- 1/4 cup beaten egg or egg substitute (optional)

Preparation:
Soak raisins in hot water or room temperature bourbon/rum for a minimum of 20 minutes to 1 hour (an hour for full bourbon/rum flavor in the fruit). You can start them much earlier if you want, but the bourbon/rum flavor will be stronger

if you do. (Don't worry: the alcohol burns off during baking so you won't be loopy when you eat the pie—unless you've been helping yourself to the soaked raisins.)

Clean, peel, and slice the apples into thin (but not paper thin) slices. Sprinkle with lemon juice to avoid discoloration.

Prepare pie dish with crust and set aside.

Preheat oven to 425 degrees F.

In a large cup or medium bowl, mix all dry ingredients: sugar(s) flour, salt, spices, nuts, pepper. Use 4 Tablespoons of flour if the raisins have been soaked in alcohol or the apples are producing a lot of juice. Less if the apples are dry or the raisins have been soaked in water.

Drain the raisins and add to apples.

In an extra-large bowl, mix dry ingredients with apples and raisins, plus any juice the apples have produced, until the apples are thoroughly and evenly coated with the sugar/spice/flour mixture.

Arrange the filling in prepared pie crust so the apple slices are densely packed (to minimize collapsing during baking.) Scrape and pour any juice or syrup that has formed in the bowl over the top of the apples. If you have used bourbon/rum to soak the raisins, dot the apples with butter before putting on the top crust. Otherwise, apply the top crust and seal to bottom crust and pierce upper crust several times with a sharp knife to let the steam out. Brush top crust with beaten egg and a sprinkle of white sugar, if desired.

Bake at 425 degrees for 35-45 minutes or until crust is golden. Let stand at room temperature at least 20 minutes before serving.

Notes: Brown sugar, alcohol-soaked raisins, and butter will all change the taste and final character of the pie, so feel free to adjust to your taste. I find that the pie tastes richer if you include butter with the bourbon raisins, but you won't miss it if you don't put it on. The pie has a nicely tart taste with a bit of bite, but not too much and more complex flavor than you may expect from a traditional American dessert.

Greek Butter Cookies (Kourabiethes)
Jeffrey Sigger

These are traditional cookies made in Greek homes during the Christmas Holidays, but they're popular year round.

Ingredients to make approximately 3-dozen:
1 cup unsalted butter
4 cups confectioners' sugar
1 egg yolk
1 tablespoons brandy
3 cups flour (may need more)
1/2 teaspoons baking powder
1 teaspoons almond extract
1/2-3/4 cups chopped and toasted almonds
36 whole cloves (enough for 1 per cookie)
2 greased cookie sheets

Instructions:
Sift flour together with baking powder and set aside.
Mix butter with sugar until it is very fluffy and light. Add the egg yolk, extract and brandy.
Slowly add the sifted flour and baking powder. Add more if necessary. The dough is done when you can work with it without it sticking to your fingers.
Lastly, add the toasted almonds.
Form dough into small balls (walnut size) or crescents and place them onto the lightly greased baking sheets. Insert one clove into the center of each ball/crescent.
Bake in a moderate oven (350F/170C) for approximately 20 minutes (a bit less if you use a confection oven).
Roll the cookies, while warm, in confectioners' sugar and then place them on a rack to cool. Sift more confectioners' sugar over them; they should be drowning in the sugar!

When cool, store them in tin or glass containers. They keep well.

Enjoy!

NOTE: Recipe unabashedly stolen from Rounces Apostolou of Hotel Mykonos Adonis.

Schmidt Ginger Cookies
A Mrs. Crimespree favorite
Bryan VanMeter

Ingredients:
- 2 cups sugar
- 1 cups molasses
- 2 eggs
- 1 cups lard or shortening
- 3 teaspoons baking soda
- 1 teaspoons cinnamon
- 1 teaspoons vanilla
- 2 teaspoons ginger
- 1/2 teaspoons cloves
- 4 cups flour

Preparation:
Mix all ingredients. Chill dough for 2 hours. Roll into small balls about the size of a walnut and dip in sugar. Place in a 375 degree oven for 10-12 minutes or until the tops Crack.

Note: I use colored sugar for different holidays. These are an old family recipe and the best ginger cookies I've ever had

Recipe for Chocolate Fudge Cake
Reba Dorman White

In the small North Carolina town where I spent much of my childhood, cooking, especially baking and desserts, was taken very seriously. Many of the women had specialties for which they were well-known. My Aunt Vera's specialties were apple pie and oatmeal cookies. My cousins were lemon cake, spice cake, chocolate fudge, and Divinity fudge. A family friend made a Japanese fruitcake, which was neither Japanese nor a fruitcake, but it was delicious.

Everyone shared both the sweets themselves, and the recipes. Most of the recipes had originated in a cookbook, a magazine, or a label, like the Toll House cookie recipe on the Nestlé bag. But the cooks changed them, added to them, and made them from memory, no longer looking at the recipes, and may no longer remember where they got the recipe.

My family loved chocolate, so my mother prepared all kinds of chocolate goodies, but she was famous for her fudge cake. The source of the original recipe is no longer certain. It may have appeared on a Crisco label, but more likely, it came from a Softasilk label, or someone gave it to her. Or perhaps it came from General Foods's 1932 cookbook, where I found a version.

Ingredients:
- 1 cups boiling water
- 4 square (4 ounces) unsweetened chocolate, cut into small pieces
- 2 1/4 cup sifted cake flour
- 2 cups sugar
- 1/2 teaspoons baking powder
- 1 teaspoons baking soda
- 1/2 teaspoons salt
- 1/2 cups Crisco

1/2 cups buttermilk
1 teaspoons vanilla
2 eggs, well beaten

Stir boiling water and chocolate until chocolate melts. Cool. Sift flour, sugar, baking powder, soda and salt together. Stir into chocolate mixture. Add Crisco. Beat about 1 minute in an electric mixer at medium speed. Scrape bowl constantly while beating. Add buttermilk, vanilla and eggs. Beat again, scraping bowl. Pour into greased 9x13-inch pan (I line mine with wax paper). Cook 45 minutes in preheated 350 degree oven. Cool and frost.

1 Minute Fudge Frosting:
    4 squares (4 ounces) unsweetened chocolate, cut fine
    3 cups sugar
    14 tablespoons milk
    4 tablespoons Crisco
    4 tablespoons butter
    2 tablespoons corn syrup
    1/2 teaspoons salt
    2 teaspoons vanilla

Place chocolate, milk, sugar, Crisco, butter, syrup and salt in saucepan. Bring slowly to a full boil stirring constantly, boil briskly 1 minute. Cool to lukewarm, add vanilla and beat until thick enough to spread. If frosting becomes too thick, add a little cream or soften over hot water. (I add a cup of chopped pecans.)

This makes enough to thickly frost top and sides of a 9x13-inch cake.

Mojito Cupcakes
Lois Winston

In my Anastasia Pollack Crafting Mystery series, magazine crafts editor and reluctant amateur sleuth Anastasia Pollack juggles recent widowhood, two teenage sons, a semi-invalid communist mother-in-law, her Russian princess mother, a mountain of debt, and the occasional dead body. She rarely has time for breakfast and often skips lunch. Luckily, food editor Cloris McWerther keeps her nourished with baked goods. In Decoupage Can Be Deadly, the fourth book in the series, Anastasia mulls over whodunit while savoring mojito cupcakes.—Lois Winston, USA Today bestselling author

Yield: 2 dozen cupcakes

Ingredients:
    1 box white cake mix
    2 cups water
    2 tablespoons vegetable oil
    3 large egg whites
    1 lime, juiced (reserve 3 tablespoons)
    2 tablespoons lime zest
    1 teaspoon rum extract
    4 1/2 tablespoons rum
    3 tablespoons brown sugar
    1 1/2 teaspoon mint extract
    4 cups confectioner's sugar, sifted
    6 tablespoons butter, softened
    1/4 cup milk
    Mint leaves (optional)

Preparation:
Preheat oven to 350 degrees F.

COOKING WITH CRIMESPREE

Mix together 1 1/3 cups water, oil, egg whites, lime juice (minus the 3 reserved tablespoons,) zest, and rum extract. Fold into cake mix. Beat at medium speed for 2 minutes.

Scoop batter into paper-lined muffin tins, filling each about 2/3 full. Bake 18-24 minutes.

Mix rum, 2 tablespoons lime juice, brown sugar and mint extract together in saucepan. Simmer 5 minutes.

Poke a few holes in top of cupcakes. Pour syrup into holes. Allow cupcakes to cool completely.

For frosting, mix together confectioner's sugar, butter, 2/3 cup water, and 1 tablespoon lime juice. If frosting is too watery, add more confectioners' sugar; if too thick, add more water. Frost cooled cupcakes. Decorate with mint leaf.

Mum's Sherry Trifle Recipe
Simon Wood

For Cake:
    Enough large pieces of sponge cake, jelly roll, ladyfingers or pound cake to line the bottom of a 9-inch glass dish
    Raspberry jam (approximately 1 cup)
    6 tablespoons sherry (or more if you like)

For custard:
    1 pint milk
    2 ounces cream
    4 egg yolks
    1 ounce sugar (about 7 teaspoons)
    2 tablespoons cornstarch
    1 vanilla pod, split and seeds removed (or 1 teaspoons vanilla extract)

For decoration:
    1/2 pint of heavy cream
    Toasted, sliced almonds, sliced fruit or other garnish

Preparation:
Spread some jam on each piece of cake and place in the bottom of a large glass dish or bowl. (You can melt the jam a bit first to make it easier to spread). If you're using a jelly roll, skip the jam, and cut the jelly roll into 1 1/2 inches to 2 inches thick "rounds".

Pour the sherry evenly over the cake pieces and let absorb for a few minutes.

In a heavy bottomed saucepan place the milk and cream and 1 teaspoons of the sugar, bring to a gentle simmer, once simmering, turn the heat to its lowest.

In a large heat proof bowl, place the sugar, cornstarch and the egg yolks and with a hand whisk, whisk until light, creamy and paler in color.

Slowly, while still whisking, pour the warmed milk into the egg mixture.

Strain the custard sauce through a fine sieve, back into the saucepan, add the seeds from the vanilla pod. Over a low heat, stir constantly and gradually until the custard begins to thicken. Careful not to boil or let burn. (Note: if using vanilla extract instead of the vanilla bean, add near the end)

Finally, once thickened enough to coat the back of a spoon, remove from the heat, pour over the cake and allow to cool.

While custard is cooling, whip 1/2 pint of heavy cream until soft peaks form.

Spread whipped cream over custard layer and garnish with toasted almonds or fruit. Chill 2 hours before serving.

Southern Chocolate Chess Pie
Tom Young

Ingredients:
    1 1/4 cup sugar
    2 heaping spoonfuls of cocoa
    1 cup of evaporated milk
    2 eggs, beaten
    1 teaspoon of vanilla
    2 tablespoons of melted butter
    1 pie shell

This is way too easy: Mix everything in a food processor. Pour it into the pie shell. Bake at 350 degrees for about 45 minutes. Tell everybody you worked hard on it for hours.

BEVERAGES
Most with alcohol

"Merry met, and merry part, I drink to thee with all my heart"
—anonymous

How to Make Tea
SJ Rozan

I know. You're thinking, Seriously, SJ? Are you so rarefied—or are your cooking skills so non-existent—that this is all you can come up with?

On the first: rarefied? Have you met me? On the second: sort of. I don't cook, so asking me for a recipe is folly from the start. However, I do drink a lot of tea. As do Lydia Chin and her mom. One thing that irritates all three of us is a bad cup of tea. So for those of you who'd like to try the tea experience, or have tried it and found it wanting, here is the right way to go about it.

Step One: Use a clean pot the right size for your tea. Probably you're not going to try to make four cups of tea in a two-cup pot and if you are there's very little I can do for you. But don't do it the other way, either. Tea likes to fit snugly. Use a small pot for a cup or two, a large pot if you're serving guests. Make sure it's clean. Don't just rinse it after each use, wash it. Tea is notoriously clingy and eventually you won't be able to tell your Assam from your Elderberry.

Exception: if you're using an unglazed clay pot—one of the famous Yixing pots, for example—never use soap. Just rinse; but the secret of an unglazed pot is, you must commit each pot to a specific kind of tea and use only that tea in that pot. By which I do not mean, this pot for black tea, that pot for green tea. I mean, this pot for Kenyan Tinderet, that pot for Yunnan. Tea flavors the unglazed pot. My advice? Stick with glass or glazed pots.

Step Two: Use good tea. Honestly, all three of us (SJ, LC, and LC's mom) find Lipton's at the absolute outer edge of drinkability. Twining's, better; Red Rose or Tetley's, never. But for really good tea, use really good tea. Buy it loose, from a specialty coffee-and-tea purveyor.

Something important to know about tea: Tea comes from the camellia sinensis plant. If it comes from there it's tea, if it doesn't, it's not. That elderberry I mentioned before, it's not properly a tea, it's a tisane. ("Miss Lemon! My tisane, if you please!") However, I have a feeling that ship's sailed. Everyone refers to any plant part steeped in hot water as "tea" these days. That's okay with me; but why, then, do I bring it up? Because actual teas, that is, everything made from camellia sinensis, differ in only two ways: what they take from the soil and weather of the places where they're grown; and how long they're aged. The first is what makes Yunnan different from Assam. The second is what makes green tea different from black tea.

Tea leaves are picked and then dried. Barely dried, it's white tea. Left a little longer, it's green; and so on through oolong, red, black, and those killer teas like Pu-erh at the end of the spectrum. It's all the same stuff.

Step Three: This is the most important part, and for most people just coming into the world of tea, the most poorly understood. Remember this rule: the lighter the tea, the more tea and the less time. Green tea, for example: you'll need a heaping teaspoon of tea per person, or more if you like stronger tea. But never brew green tea for more than sixty seconds. Never. It'll just get bitter. Some of the best green teas you can pour a second pot of water over after you've poured the first cup out, and the tea will brew again, another cup as good. But don't let that first cup sit in the water more than sixty seconds. You'll thank me. For oolongs, that would be two minutes; for dark teas like Yunnan or Kenyan Tinderet, three and a half or four. Remember: Want it stronger, use more tea. Brew it longer, get bitter tea.

Step Four: For the dark teas, bring the water to a rolling boil but don't let it keep boiling before you pour it into the pot. The oxygen will boil out and the tea will taste metallic. For green and white teas, stop it just before it boils.

Step Five: Of course, use cups or mugs, never paper or—horrors—Styrofoam. Milk or sugar? Honey? To taste, but milk only in the dark teas. Anything from oolong to white, no milk; they're all slightly acidic and milk will just make them taste foul. Sugar, honey, agave, whatever you like, in any tea you want to put it in. The Brits put the milk in the cup first, then the tea, then the sugar, but I've never known what that milk-first thing buys you. Personally, I use milk in dark tea but no sugar in any tea.

And there you are. Two pages of directions on making tea. But if you've been wondering what the whole tea thing is about, or if you've been disappointed in tea is the past, try doing it this way. Enjoy yourself!

Long Beach Iced Tea for Two
Anonymous-9

Ingredients:
- 2 cups ice cubes
- 1 ounce vodka
- 1 ounce gin
- 1 ounce white rum
- 1 ounce tequila
- 1 ounce Grand Marnier or Cointreau
- 1 tablespoon fresh lemon juice
- 1 tablespoon fresh lime juice
- 1/2 cup cola, or to taste
- Fresh lemon and lime wedges

Directions:
Fill a cocktail shaker with ice. Pour the vodka, gin, rum, tequila, liqueur, and juices into the shaker. Cover and shake vigorously to combine and chill. Pour the mixture, ice and all, into 2 glasses or beer mugs and top off with cola. Garnish with wedges and serve.

Anonymous-9 is the author of the Hard Bite series, published by Blasted Heath, New Pulp Press, and Down & Out Books.

Sour Cherry Mojito
James Benn

Ingredients:
 1 tablespoon raw sugar
 9 mint leaves
 Juice of 1 lime
 3 ounces white rum
 Ice cubes
 Dash of club soda or sparkling water
 Dash or 2 of Triple Sec
 Handful of pitted sour cherries (and any juice resulting from the pitting process)

Preparation:
Place 6 mint leaves in a tall glass. Add the sugar. Muddle same. Toss in the cherries, muddle more.

Add the lime juice, white rum, triple sec and ice. You can mix well in the glass or transfer to a cocktail shaker and shake it up.

Pour the beverage back in your glass, add dash of club soda or sparkling water. Garnish with the remaining mint leaves.

Drink. Make another. Repeat as necessary.

Bourbon Slush
Christy Campbell

Ingredients:
- 1 (12 ounces) container of frozen OJ
- 1 (12 ounces) container of frozen lemonade
- 1 1/2 cup sugar
- 1 1/2 cups Makers Mark (there is no other bourbon!)
- 2 cups strong tea
- 7 cups water

Preparation:
First brew 2 cups of strong tea. Let it cool a little. Next mix all ingredients in a freezer friendly container. Let it sit in freezer overnight. When you are ready for a drink, scoop the frozen mixture of the gods in a KY Derby glass (of Highball glass) and add a splash of sprite and a cherry for decoration!

Thriller Tequila
Marcia Clark

One of my favorite summer drinks:
To make a pitcher that serves XXX number of people—I can't say how many because it depends on whether your friends are heavy drinkers:
- 2 cups Patron Silver tequila
- 3/4 cup fresh lime juice
- 1 sliced cucumber—or 2 if you're using Persian cucumbers
- 2 cleaned, sliced jalapeno peppers

Let it soak for a couple of hours, then strain it, add agave nectar to taste—and I like to add sparkling water but that's a matter of preference—and pour over ice.

Sub-lime Summer Chiller
Alison Gaylin

I like a good Scotch as much as the next crime writer. But when upstate New York gets humid and buggy, a good gin drink is always the best defense. I threw this cocktail together on a hot summer night when I realized we were low on tonic. It's light, refreshing and not at all sweet—everything I like in a summer drink.

Ingredients:
    4 shots gin
    1 medium cucumber
    3-4 limes
    Seltzer water
    Ice

Instructions (makes two drinks):
Liquify and strain the cucumber, leaving a few slices for garnish.
Juice the limes.
In a shaker, combine ice, gin, cucumber juice and lime juice.
Shake well.
Pour the mixture into tumblers with ice, top off with seltzer water, garnish with cucumber slices.
Enjoy!

The Post Day O' Writing Meal
Gregg Hurwitz

1. Take out a rocks glass.
2. Plink in one purified square or sphere ice cube.
3. Pour in two fingers of Blanton's bourbon.
4. Sip soothingly.

Oatmeal Cookie Martini
Ruth Jordan

Who says you cannot drink dessert? Never a fan of the sweet cocktails this drink has become legendary at Castle Crimespree. Discovered on the mean streets of Williamsburg, VA, it has been Mrs. Crimespree tweaked. Made in both small and large batches the following recipe is given in parts. It will be a favorite.

Ingredients:
    2 parts Jägermeister
    2 parts Baileys' Irish Cream
    1 parts Butterscotch Schnapps
    1/3 part Goldschläger

Pour all ingredients over ice in a shaker. Shake strongly for a minute. Pour into martini glass. You can dress it fancy if you like. Swirl cinnamon on top or add raisins skewered on a swizzle stick. Raisins soaked in dark rum are even better.

My Ernest Hemingway Mojito
Craig McDonald

Ingredients:
  6 fresh mint sprigs
  1 ounces lime juice
  3/4 ounces simple syrup
  2 ounces light rum
  Lime wedge

How to:
"Crush 5 mint sprigs into the bottom of a chilled highball glass. Pour in lime juice, simple syrup, and rum. Fill glass with crushed ice, and stir gently. Garnish with lime wedge and remaining mint sprig. Sometimes a splash of club soda is added."

Stevens Summer Breeze
Taylor Stevens

Ingredients:
- 1 ounces Deep Eddy Ruby Red vodka (this is a grapefruit infused vodka)
- 1 ounces silver tequila
- 2 ounces watermelon juice (fresh from a watermelon)

Add with crushed ice to shaker and shake well. Transfer to glass and, depending on your sweet tooth, top with club soda, ginger ale, or sprite.

OTHER TITLES FROM DOWN AND OUT BOOKS

See www.DownAndOutBooks.com for complete list

By Anonymous-9
Bite Hard

By J.L. Abramo
Catching Water in a Net
Clutching at Straws
Counting to Infinity
Gravesend
Chasing Charlie Chan
Circling the Runway (*)

By Trey R. Barker
2,000 Miles to Open Road
Road Gig: A Novella
Exit Blood
Death is Not Forever (*)

By Richard Barre
The Innocents
Bearing Secrets
Christmas Stories
The Ghosts of Morning
Blackheart Highway
Burning Moon
Echo Bay
Lost

By Eric Beetner and JB Kohl
Over Their Heads (*)

By Eric Beetner and Frank Scalise
The Backlist (*)

By Rob Brunet
Stinking Rich

By Milton T. Burton
Texas Noir

By Dana Cameron (editor)
Murder at the Beach: Bouchercon Anthology 2014

By Tom Crowley
Vipers Tail
Murder in the Slaughterhouse

By Frank De Blase
Pine Box for a Pin-Up
Busted Valentines and Other Dark Delights
A Cougar's Kiss (*)

By Les Edgerton
The Genuine, Imitation, Plastic Kidnapping

By A.C. Frieden
Tranquility Denied
The Serpent's Game
The Pyongyang Option (*)

By Jack Getze
Big Numbers
Big Money
Big Mojo

By Keith Gilman
Bad Habits

(*)—Coming Soon

OTHER TITLES FROM DOWN AND OUT BOOKS

See www.DownAndOutBooks.com for complete list

By William Hastings (editor)
Stray Dogs: Writing from the Other America

By Matt Hilton
No Going Back (*)
Rules of Honor (*)
The Lawless Kind (*)

By Terry Holland
An Ice Cold Paradise
Chicago Shiver

By Darrel James, Linda O. Johnston & Tammy Kaehler (editors)
Last Exit to Murder

By David Housewright & Renée Valois
The Devil and the Diva

By David Housewright
Finders Keepers
Full House

By Jon Jordan
Interrogations

By Jon & Ruth Jordan (editors)
Murder and Mayhem in Muskego

By Bill Moody
Czechmate
The Man in Red Square
Solo Hand
The Death of a Tenor Man
The Sound of the Trumpet
Bird Lives!

By Gary Phillips
The Perpetrators
Scoundrels (Editor)
Treacherous

By Gary Phillips, Tony Chavira & Manoel Maglhaes
Beat L.A. (Graphic Novel)

By Robert J. Randisi
Upon My Soul
Souls of the Dead (*)
Envy the Dead (*)

By Lono Waiwaiole
Wiley's Lament
Wiley's Shuffle
Wiley's Refrain
Dark Paradise

By Vincent Zandri
Moonlight Weeps

(*)—Coming Soon

www.ingramcontent.com/pod-product-compliance
Lightning Source LLC
Chambersburg PA
CBHW020358080526
44584CB00014B/1071